Great Fishing Adventures

Great Fishing Adventures

Complete Angler's Library™
North American Fishing Club
Minneapolis, Minnesota

Great Fishing Adventures

Copyright © 1990, North American Fishing Club

Library of Congress Catalog Card Number 90-63130
ISBN 0-914697-35-8

Printed in U.S.A.
4   5   6   7   8   9

The North American Fishing Club
offers a line of hats for fishermen.
For information, write:
North American Fishing Club
P.O. Box 3403
Minneapolis, MN 55343

Contents

Saltwater Adventures

Acknowledgments

Illustrations in *Great Fishing Adventures* were created by artist Peter Ring. Cover art was created by Virgil Beck.

Special thanks to the fishermen who shared their true adventures with writers W. Horace Carter and Don Mann. Thanks also to Bob McNally, Paul Brinkman and Bill Munro who helped provide facts to the authors.

A great big thank you to the staff of the North American Fishing Club: Editor and Publisher Mark LaBarbera, Managing Editor Steve Pennaz, Associate Editors Kurt Beckstrom and Ron Larsen, Editorial Assistant Jane Boers and Layout Artist Dean Peters. Thanks also to Vice President of Products Marketing Mike Vail, Marketing Manager Linda Kalinowski and Marketing Project Coordinator Laura Resnik.

Jay Michael Strangis
Managing Editor
Complete Angler's Library

About The Authors

When it comes to freshwater fishing, co-author W. Horace Carter has seen it all. A world traveler, Horace has visited 41 foreign countries and all 50 U.S. States in search of hunting and fishing experiences. He is a popular lecturer on fishing topics at outdoor shows and fishing clubs, and a prolific writer on the subject. Horace has authored 13 books on the outdoors in the past 16 years, including a title which won first place in the Southeastern Outdoor Press Association book competition in 1988.

As an active member of the Outdoor Writers Association of America, Horace has served six years on the group's board of directors, and is the only member of this large and distinguished group of writers to have earned a Pulitzer Prize, awarded in 1953. He also served three consecutive terms as president of the Florida Outdoor Writers Association, and is a past president and current board member of the Southeastern Outdoor Press Association.

Horace writes and sells more than 200 magazine articles a year with total sales of more than 2,000 articles since 1977. He also writes two columns per week for The Tabor City (N.C.) Tribune which he owns. A company he founded, Atlantic Publishing Company, publishes hunting and fishing books.

In 1954, he was named one of the Ten Most Outstanding Young Men in America by the U.S. Junior Chamber of Commerce. He's a graduate of the University of North Carolina at Chapel Hill School of Journalism.

He was introduced to hunting and fishing as an 11-year-old in central North Carolina, and has remained an avid hunter and fisherman all of his life. Horace now lives in Cross Creek, a community totaling 200 residents, in central Florida where area lakes are known for their trophy largemouth bass and platter-sized sunfish. He serves as a panfish guide in that area while continuing his writing activities.

Co-author Don Mann is a doer as well as an observer of saltwater fishing. This accomplished writer happens to be a world-class big game fisherman. Don captured a spot in the 1989 Guinness Book of Records for catching all nine of the species of billfish recognized by the International Game Fish Association in less than one year.

Among Don's noteworthy individual catches was the 810-pound Pacific blue marlin, taken on 80-pound test line near Manta, Ecuador, in 1987. At the time, it was the second largest blue taken off the coast of Ecuador, qualifying him for membership in the prestigious 10-to-1 Club.

As a contributing editor, Don writes a monthly column covering saltwater fishing tournaments in Florida Sportsman Magazine. He also writes a regular fishing tackle column for Marlin Magazine, and numerous feature articles for other outdoor magazines.

His stories and photos appear regularly covering such diverse outdoor subjects as boating, hunting, fishing, travel and cooking. Currently, however, he is devoting most of his writing efforts to the subjects of travel and saltwater fishing, particularly trophy big game fishing.

Don has received many awards for both writing and photojournalism from the Florida Outdoor Writers Association, the Outdoor Writers Association of America and the Florida Magazine Association, as well as being the recipient of the Mako Marine Outdoor Writer of the Year Award. Several of his photos

have appeared as outdoor magazine covers.

A 1951 graduate of Princeton University, Don began writing in the mid-50s when he was a frequent contributor to Skin Diver Magazine. At the time, he was president of one of the first and largest scuba diving clubs in the country, and helped develop the first scuba training program in the United States for the Y.M.C.A. So, you could say he knows the water from top to bottom.

In the 70s, Don began concentrating his efforts in fishing and boating. He joined the Florida Sportsman Magazine staff as the boating editor in 1976 and then became the assistant editor in 1980. He serves as a member of the board of directors of the Florida Outdoor Writers Association, and is a member of the Miami Rod and Reel Club.

Don divides his time between his outdoor writing and travels to exotic fishing locations with his wife of 33 years, Daphne.

Foreword

A bolt of lightning ripped across the arctic sky, awakening me from a deliciously deep sleep. I rolled over in an attempt to get a bit more shut-eye, but a much-nearer bolt and its accompanying thunderclap squashed my attempt. Frustrated, I reached for my watch. It was nearly 4:30.

"It doesn't look like we'll get much fishing in today," sighed my fishing partner Jerold.

"I didn't think you were awake," I responded as another bolt lit the room. Across the room Jerold lay staring at the ceiling with his hands folded behind his head.

"Doesn't look like it's going to quit any time soon either," he theorized as he looked out the window and saw the storm roll across the tundra. "Guess the lake trout will have to wait another day while we ride this one out."

The rest of the camp was in the dining room when Jerold and I arrived a couple hours later. Most had already finished eating and were nursing cups of steaming coffee while staring at wild Mackay Lake. The storm had passed, but gale-force winds were still whipping the lake into a froth. Seven- to eight-foot waves pounded into the rocks below the lodge, sending spray at least a dozen feet into the air. Fishing was out of the question.

Faced with a lazy day, most of us headed for the camp lounge which comes complete with a fireplace and a remarkable number of books. I was delighted. I love to read, but rarely have the time to do so. This was a perfect opportunity.

A cozy fire was crackling in the fireplace as I headed over to the book shelf and began scanning the titles. Most of the books were cheap serial westerns with a few Tom Clancy-type suspense novels sprinkled in. Not great literature by any means, but good books for rainy days in the Northwest Territories. I removed one of the westerns from the shelf, then quickly replaced it when I spotted an old hardcover that read *Anthology Of Fishing Adventures* in faded gold lettering. Glancing over the table of contents while heading over to an overstuffed chair in front of the fireplace, I noticed the book contained fishing adventure stories from all over the world. I turned to chapter one and spent an enjoyable morning reliving the fishing adventures of sportsmen and women from two generations ago. The wind and rain were forgotten.

If there is one common thread among the world's fishermen, it's their love of telling stories. It doesn't matter if you're a bass man, a trout aficionado or someone who really enjoys the thrill of fishing monster sharks and billfish in the oceans of the world, it's a safe bet that you have heard great fishing tales, and probably have even told a few of your own.

NAFC's *Great Fishing Adventures* is the result of months of hard work. We scoured the world for the best, most interesting true fishing adventures available, then hired Don Mann and W. Horace Carter, two writers who know their stuff, to write them in the tradition of the greatest adventure writers of all time. These two men succeeded in doing just that.

Some of the stories in this book will make you shudder, others will tug on your heart and a few will make you think about your own safety the next time you head out fishing. Death is not the central theme of this book, but it is always lurking in the shadows.

Fishing, as a rule, is a very safe sport, one that can be enjoyed by the whole family. But there are times when Mother Nature seems to go berserk and wants nothing more than to claim the lives of the unprepared—and the unlucky. All the stories in this book are true and, with a little help from the authors, told by the men and women who lived them.

NAFC's *Great Fishing Adventures* has this purpose: to provide you with pure reading entertainment; something to reach for on those days when you can't get on the water yourself. Save it for a rainy day, or when the snow is so deep that it seems impossible summer will ever return. Also, the true stories in this book remind all of us that fishing can be serious business. Remember to play it safe when on the water, because there are a lot of people counting on your return. Finally, I hope you enjoy these adventure stories as much as I have.

Steve Pennaz
Executive Director
North American Fishing Club

Freshwater
Adventures

1

Bustard Islands Shipwreck

by Larry Henderson

Strong winds were kicking up whitecaps on the Bad River when I shoved off and headed toward the whitewater rapids that poured through the narrows before opening up into Georgian Bay. I was starting out from Bad River Lodge, which I operated for fishermen in Alban, Ontario, Canada. It was time to shutter up for the winter, and I had to get my fishing boats to a storage marina 18 miles upstream on Lake Huron's Georgian Bay. The November day was bitterly cold.

We had closed the lodge to clients. I was left alone to get the boats in storage and lock up the camp. We wouldn't open again until the next spring. My largest boat, a taxi-transport craft about 20 feet long, hadn't been running well so I decided to tow it with my 14-foot, cedar strip boat that was in good condition. It was like David and Goliath, but that seemed like the most practical way to get the ailing boat to the marina for repairs.

As I approached the churning water narrows I saw little risk. I had boated these rapids many times before, and was quite an accomplished boatsman. My clients had often been lost in the fog, or caught in rough winds and forced to tie up on shore. I always went to their rescue. We never had a fatality or serious injury during the 12 years we operated the Bad River Lodge, (I still operate several fishing outposts on the Bad River) but I had not counted on the extra drag of the big boat.

Before leaving home for the trek up the river, I told my wife that I was going to take the boats to the marina through the rapids.

I asked her to meet me in the afternoon back at the lodge.

I hadn't expected the rivermouth to live up to its name like it did that fateful morning. The rapids were wild, and when I eye-balled the water cascading over and around the rocks, I knew I could never tow the big boat through the hazardous narrows.

Instead, I decided to bypass them by taking a longer route on the Key River and through Georgian Bay. That change of heart almost cost my life, but at that moment I felt like I could fight the bitter wind and cold better in the open bay. It didn't cross my mind to radio the change of route to my wife. Forgetting that de-tail was stupid, multiplying my mistakes. I suppose the fact that I had made this trip so many times previously without incident lulled me into careless complacency.

It took some effort, but I motored up the Key River to a launching ramp where I left the big boat. I planned to retrieve it later and trailer it to the marina. Happy to be rid of my burden, I headed out into Georgian Bay in the tiny strip boat. It pitched in the swells, but I could handle it. At least I wouldn't have to nego-tiate the dangerous rapids that I bypassed.

About 5 p.m., with dusk settling over Georgian Bay, a heavy snow began to fall. The gusty winds became steady and quickly whipped the snowflakes into a real blizzard.

I looked at Bear, my big Newfoundland Labrador crossbreed. He was acting like a pilot in the bow of the boat, his nose pointing into the gale-force winds, blinking against the snow. I had never seen him appear so nervous in a boat before, although he fre-quently went with me when I was fishing or guiding on the Bad River.

The little boat dived and rolled precariously in the head-high breakers as we slowly moved along the archipelago of rocky out-croppings known as the Bustard Islands. There are dozens of these island rock formations in Georgian Bay. They stretch for miles, have no trees, and are home to only big boulders and birds.

Suddenly, a giant wave broke over the gunnels, flooding the boat. Bear knew we were in trouble at the same moment I did. We had to get ashore quickly or we would be in the water hanging on the side of the little boat, and drifting to God knows where.

Thankful that the outboard was still putt-putting, I headed for the nearest rocky island, a few hundred yards away. If the engine conked out, we were in real trouble. I pulled up to the boulder-

Complete Angler's Library

cluttered shore, and jumped for the nearest rock. It was slick as glass with a coating of clear ice that hadn't been apparent from the boat. I fell backward into the waist-deep surf, struggled to my feet, and saw Bear floundering alongside. I grabbed his collar, and together we dragged ourselves onto the slippery rocks. The swamped boat made a couple of fast turns in the current, then was washed out into the bay.

While most of these islands are barren, I had picked this one because it had an unmanned lighthouse. At least we could get a little protection from the vicious elements. With a wind-chill factor of 40 below, no one could survive the terrible cold on this half-acre of rocks.

Drenched from my fall into the lake, I was freezing. Bear shook the water from his slick coat and except for the ice crystals in his hair, he didn't seem to be suffering from the cold and wind like I was.

As darkness crept over the rocks, survival depended upon my resourcefulness. I looked up at the green signal light burning 35 feet above my head. The only way to get into the lighthouse was by climbing the narrow wooden ladder all the way to an entrance near the top.

I put Bear over my shoulder and began the climb. The biting wind and icy cold challenged every muscle in my body. But I knew that if I didn't make it to the top of the lighthouse it was curtains for me and Bear.

My hunting clothes had frozen stiff and I was shaking from the cold, but we made it. I pushed Bear through the opening where the green light shone and climbed in with him. The light didn't give much heat, but anything beat the crashing waves and sheets of snow outside.

I took inventory. The only things I had were five cigarettes and a lighter. The cigarettes were so wet that I feared they would disintegrate. The lighter was soaked and useless. But I balanced them on the big bulb of the light. It took some time, but eventually the lighter worked, and the cigarettes could be smoked. It wasn't a bonanza but it sure boosted my spirits.

With my whereabouts unknown, shivering with the cold and growing hungrier by the minute, my future seemed mighty limited. If we had saved a fish hook or two from the boat, maybe we could catch a walleye, bass or pike when morning came. But we had saved nothing of any value to man or dog.

Dogs can stand cold much better than humans. I cuddled up to Bear, and he seemed to welcome the close association. I'm certain his body heat kept me from a hypothermic death that night, though not from a miserable eight hours of suffering.

Dawn broke the next morning, and I knew there would be no rescue effort that day. The whole bay was white with driving snow as the blizzard howled on. Visibility was only a few yards, and it had grown colder. I conjectured that my strip boat may have washed up on a shore somewhere, and it would be a good indication that I was drowned. They might not even search for me, assuming that I had fallen overboard during the storm.

By the second day our stomachs were growling with hunger. I was losing hope. The weather had not abated. If there were any rescue efforts made they were sure to be minimal. I stayed alive by hugging Bear day and night. His body heat was a blessing.

I prayed for a rescue. I have always believed in a Supreme Being, and I spent a lot of time talking to Him in that lighthouse. I talked with a lot of other people too. My two children and wife were constantly on my mind. I told them over and over that I hoped I had been a good father and husband.

By the time the third morning arrived, Bear and I were looking at each other with cannibalistic thoughts. Hunger can do a lot to a man or dog's mind after three starving days in frigid weather.

Finally, the blizzard blew itself out. The skies cleared and I stepped out on the lighthouse ledge. I could see search planes working all along the river and shoreline where I had planned my original course. It was logical to think the rapids on the river caused my trouble. My many pilot friends were searching frantically for me. I could see them clearly six miles away. There was nothing I could do that would help them find me. There weren't even any sticks on the island that I could use to make a fire.

Bear and I anguished all day watching the faraway search. Once a plane wandered off from the river search, and flew directly over us, raising my hopes. The plane's pontoons straddled the lighthouse. I jumped and waved frantically on the narrow lighthouse ledge. But the pilot couldn't see me. You cannot see straight down and directly in front of an aircraft. After a few minutes, the plane droned out of sight.

In the afternoon, the Ontario Provincial Police helicopter

crew joined in the search. At exactly 4:45 p.m. on that memorable day, with darkness again settling over the bay and the islands, a member of the helicopter crew saw me waving my yellow T-shirt from the lighthouse ledge.

Ten minutes later they hovered over the rocks, and picked up a grateful man and dog. Limited space in the helicopter necessitated one of the crew remaining on the rock while Bear and I were flown to the marina. The helicopter would quickly return for the crew member. At least his whereabouts were known.

At the marina, they brought me a huge serving of hot mashed potatoes and hamburgers. Bear got an equal portion of the same food. Needless to say, we wolfed it down. Bear wouldn't touch the coffee, but I gulped down his share of that. It seemed to warm me all the way through. I had wondered if I ever would be warm again. It is a wonderful feeling when you cheat death.

In 1989 Bear died of old age. It was like losing a dear friend. I will forever give Bear credit for saving my life, keeping me from freezing to death on that desolate rock in Georgian Bay.

I have also made a vow—I'll never go anywhere again without telling someone where I'm going. It would have saved Bear and me a lot of suffering those cold November days in 1984.

2

Dangerous Tug-O-War

by Josh Adams

S etting the hook in a big king salmon in plain view of a giant grizzly bear was my first mistake. My second was trying to wrestle the fish to the hill after 1,000 pounds of brute strength had decided the fish was his. It can easily happen on a remote Alaskan salmon stream. It happened to me on the Brooks River.

Several of us were staying at the rustic Brooks Lodge in the national park to fish from the bank of the Brooks near the Alaskan west coast. A fast jet boat had brought us two hours up the Nanek River from the tiny hamlet of King Salmon. We were warned by rangers when we stepped off the boat that less-than-friendly bears were feeding all over the area.

To emphasize the point, a ranger escorted us to the fish-dressing shack a hundred yards from the river, and showed us its strong double doors. They were bristling with fresh raw splinters.

"Last night some fishermen left fish parts in the garbage cans in this shed," the ranger said. "The grizzlies smelled them during the night and almost tore the place down trying to get inside. That's why we have double doors with inside locking devices."

He also told us that only a few days before we arrived several bears had broken into the kitchen-dining building, destroying everything inside as they ransacked the place searching for food.

Later, as we were unpacking a few things another ranger gave us further advice.

"You be sure to keep your cabin doors securely closed at night," she said, "and don't keep any meat or fish in the cabin. Grizzlies roam the yard after the lights go out, and you don't want to get caught in your cabin with a big grizzly knocking on the door."

That was the second time we had been warned of the danger of the grizzlies, and I began to wonder how safe it was to fish here in this wilderness.

When we were ready to head out another ranger gave us more instructions.

"When you hook a fish in the river the noise of the fish thrashing in the water, along with the smell when you get the salmon on the hill, will attract any grizzly in the area. Get your fish in with as little noise as possible, and then quickly put it in the large plastic bags that we provide. That reduces the chance of the bears smelling your catch. Then, don't leave your fish on the bank. Bring it in the bag across the pontoon bridge to the lodge where we can put it up for you until you get ready to dress it. You can always go back and fish some more, but don't keep a caught fish with you. That's asking for bear trouble. They like to get a meal without having to work for it."

Inexperienced in fishing with grizzlies breathing down my neck, I listened, but couldn't help wondering if these park rangers weren't a little too dramatic. Perhaps in the interest of safety they exaggerated a bit.

We rushed off to the nearby river with tackle and lures in hand. It was within rock-throwing distance of the lodge. I walked across a short pontoon bridge and selected a shoreline spot that looked like a good place to fish. Even though it was immediately adjacent to the little bridge, you could see thousands of big reddish salmon milling on the bottom as they fought the current to reach the very spot of their nativity.

Ten minutes after making my first cast, I set the hook and fought a 15-pound fish to the bank. She was far too ripe, having already turned red. Salmon are not good to eat at that stage so the catch and release had been quick. I looked around, and there was no bear in sight. The ranger must be overly protective, I rationalized. Where were those dangerous critters?

I walked a few steps up the river and cast again. I had barely started my retrieve when it balked and headed offshore. I struggled with a heavy rod and reel that doubled like a hunting bow. I had latched on to a real lunker salmon. Twice, the fish exploded

Dangerous Tug-O-War

on the surface in the shallow water, and then made two long runs toward the open water. Would she take off all my line?

I was no novice fisherman. I had landed big fish before. I fought the giant king with patience, taking in slack when I had it, and bowing to the pull when the pressure was greatest.

Slowly I recovered line with the huge fish still on the hook. I was using experience gained from a lifetime of angling all over Canada and Alaska. Even the kibitzers at my elbow were applauding my effort. They didn't know I had also fought tarpon, marlin and sailfish far to the south for years.

At that moment, I looked across the narrow river and spotted a giant grizzly lumbering into the stream. He stood erect with the water lapping under his front paws. He had heard my thrashing fish, and that meant mealtime to him.

Someone yelled, "Adams, you got a bear heading your way! You better cut the fish loose and head for home."

I saw several anglers trotting across the pontoon bridge toward the lodge and the safety of the buildings, but I was too stubborn to lose a trophy-size salmon just because a grizzly wanted it for dinner. I thought I wanted it more.

I glanced at the bear again. He was less than a hundred yards away and coming fast. Maybe I could still save my fish and beat the bear to the bridge. The grizzly was huffing and puffing from fighting the river current, and I was huffing and puffing from struggling with my fish on the line. I pumped on the rod a little more vigorously, and tightened my drag a bit. I reeled harder and faster than ever. The fish made a run for the bank, and for a moment it looked like I was winning this bout. Then he turned for the open water again and took off some more line, renewing the struggle.

"Come on, Adams. Cut the line. That bear is closing in on you fast," another angler screamed as he ran across the bridge with his tackle in hand.

The warning was too late. The grizzly saw the salmon streaking past him in the open water and dived. He surfaced a few feet away with the flapping salmon in his mouth and paws.

I made one last attempt to save my fish, yanking on it with all the power I had. But I could not break the 25-pound test monofilament nor tear the salmon away from the powerful grizzly. I only angered the dangerous creature.

The bear grabbed the strong line and jerked so hard that my

Dangerous Tug-O-War

feet went out from under me. I slid bottom-first into the shallow water, still clinging to my tackle. Scrambling to my feet, I lunged for the shore and fell again, face down. I looked up cautiously, spitting and sputtering, fully expecting that giant bear to be standing over me. He was still concentrating on the fish, but my yank on the line had made him howling mad.

He broke for the bank in a fast trot, and headed straight for me, snarling through his teeth, which were still clamped around the salmon. Luckily there was no bank to climb, just rocky shoreline. That bear would have to be a record sprinter to catch me if I didn't fall again on the loose rocks. But I had heard they could run the 100-yard dash in less than 10 seconds.

He was only 10 steps away when I fully realized the gravity of my situation. That bear could cut me off from the safety of the bridge and the lodge. Saving my salmon suddenly seemed so trivial. I threw down my rod and reel and streaked for the bridge. Even that was no safety zone as the bears frequently crossed the bridge too. But it was my only route to the security of the cabins.

The bear made one move as if to cut me off from the bridge, still hanging on to his dinner and dragging my tackle. I suppose he would have mauled me good for trying to take the salmon out of his mouth if he had caught me. But he didn't! I resembled a wet, disheveled track star near the end of a tough race, but I made it to the safety of the lodge.

Fortunately, the grizzly was more concerned with saving his meal than avenging the harassment. He didn't give chase; instead he lumbered into the shoreline jungle nonchalantly dragging my rod and reel behind him.

An hour later, a ranger and I went back to the river bank. My tackle was gone. We parted the bushes and fought through the dense thicket. Many yards away we spotted a foot-long piece of my prized graphite rod. We never found anything else. All I had for my experience was the frightening memory.

Complete Angler's Library

3

Beware Those Biting Worms

by Doyle McAfee

W hile it may turn your stomach to talk about some baits at the dinner table (like maggots and catalpa worms turned wrong side out), they are usually harmless. I have fished with almost every kind of live bait known to man, all over the country, for nearly every species of freshwater fish. And I thought I'd seen them all. That is, until I saw some biting worms.

I was smallmouth bass fishing down the precipice shoreline of Center Hill Lake a few years ago when a young man on the bank introduced them to me.

I was having absolutely no luck that day casting my most respected and productive spoon plugs for the smallies that infest these East Tennessee waters of the Caney Fork River. The Caney Fork is 64 miles of high-cliff, rocky shoreline from Rock Island to the Center Hill Lake Dam east of Nashville. There are miles of beautiful shoreline on this stretch of water, as scenic as any tangled mountain river could be. Water laces in and out of creeks and coves, filling deep mountain ravines with pure, clear water. The smallmouth bass that thrive in this excellent habitat attract anglers throughout the year.

I tried trolling at first, and when I didn't get any strikes I turned to casting into the deep water at the base of the cliffs. I'd fished the area many times before and knew that plenty of 5-pound bronzebacks were apt to suspend there awaiting an influx of shad. But I couldn't get a strike with anything in my tackle box. I was on the verge of giving up and going home to Rock Island.

"Ouch!" came a shout from atop a rocky cliff on the shoreline. I looked up and saw a teenager on the bank baiting his hook. He looked like a native. He might know how to catch these bass, I thought, and I decided to hang close and watch.

He cast out his line and almost immediately got a strike. I watched enviously as he wrestled a nice smallmouth up the cliff. Beginner's luck, I surmised. I stayed in the area, casting into the rocky holes only a short distance from where the kid was fishing, keeping an eye out just in case he caught another bass.

Not more than a few minutes had passed before I saw him struggling to reel in another fish up the high bank—even larger than the first!

I couldn't believe it. Here I was in a nice boat with all kinds of proven lures, and I couldn't buy a bite. What was his secret?

Before the kid had fished half an hour, he pulled in a third smallmouth. I was fit to be tied and inched closer to his honey hole thinking maybe he had located a big school that he would share with me. I began casting my small crankbait right in the area where he was pulling in his fish. Nothing! I twitched and reeled. Then I tried jigging off the bottom. Still it was fruitless. The bass didn't like anything I offered. I heard a splash and looked up to see the kid pulling in yet another nice fish. I couldn't stand it anymore, I had to know what his secret weapon was.

"Son," I hollered, "what are you fishing with? I can't catch a thing, and you keep right on pulling in those fine smallmouths."

"Ain't no secret, mister," he called down. "I'm using some biting worms that I caught back there in the woods."

"Biting worms? I never heard of those," I called back.

"I was digging for night crawlers, and lucked right up on a whole bunch of these wiggling worms," he said. "They'se the toughest worms I ever saw. You can't hardly get a hook through 'em, and they bite me every time I put one on a hook. But the bass sure like 'em. You want to try one?"

"I never saw any kind of fishing worms that would bite back," I said, really worried now. "Why don't you bring one down to the foot of the cliff and show him to me?"

I trolled over to a flat area on the bank to meet him. He handed me his fish bait can, with three or four of the biting worms trying to get out.

"Show me where those worms bit you," I commanded.

"They all bit this hand," he said, holding it out, "you can see the red spots, but it didn't do any more than just sting a little."

I looked at the marks scattered across his hand. "Son, you are fishing with newly-born, poisonous cottonmouth moccasins! You may be in real trouble. Where do you live?"

"A couple of miles back through the woods that way," he nodded toward the highway.

"I don't believe I ought to let you try to get that distance by

yourself. Just get in the boat and I'll take you to a doctor. I'll explain it to your folks later."

He looked a little skeptical about going off with a total stranger, but he could see I meant business. He put his humble rod and reel in the boat. I cranked the outboard and we roared down the river to the landing where I had left my car.

A half-hour later we arrived in McMinnville at the hospital emergency room. I explained the situation to the physician, and showed him the other "biting worms" in the can.

"They sure are cottonmouths," the doctor said.

He examined each of four bites on the kid's hand. Redness circled the tiny double fang marks where the vipers had struck.

"You are a mighty lucky young man," the doctor said. "These are mostly dry bites. The little snakes can poison you just like the big ones. These ones are so young though, they put very little poison in you. If they had been a few days older, we would have had to hospitalize you. You'd be hurting pretty bad right now if you had the normal amount of venom in those bites. Your hand would be swollen and you'd be nauseated. I'll give you a shot of cottonmouth antidote and I'm fairly sure you'll be all right."

We both breathed a sigh of relief and after the doctor cleaned up the kid's hand and gave him the shot, I took the young fisherman back to his home. He told his parents the whole story about the biting worms, and we both assured them that he was going to be all right. He said he'd never again go fishing with cottonmouths for bass bait. I grinned at his last remark and headed toward my car.

"Mister McAfee," he called after me, "I forgot to get the bass I caught. They're still tied out, do you want them?"

"Sure, if you don't want to go after them I could use them for supper," I replied.

"They're yours," the youngster said.

My wife and I had those bass for supper that night, and the fact that they were caught on cottonmouth biting worms didn't make them any less tasty!

4

One For The King

by Bob Ploeger

Darlene and I have been avid anglers since before we were married. Members of the North American Fishing Club, we fished mainly in the lakes and streams near our home in Sandstone, Minnesota, located halfway between Minneapolis and Duluth.

We've feasted on many a fine walleye and other local species pulled from those Midwestern waters, but that only whetted our appetite for a fishing vacation in Alaska. We listened attentively to many intriguing stories of the fantastic fishing there.

After years of planning, Darlene and I scheduled an Alaskan fishing trip. It was the culmination of a long-standing dream. Now retired, we headed north to fulfill our Alaskan fantasy in July of 1989.

We drove to Alaska from Minnesota, met our guide Dan Bishop, and planned the next day's adventure with great enthusiasm and anticipation.

At 6 a.m. on a typically overcast Alaskan day we stepped into Bishop's drift boat, a flat-bottom skiff with a pointed bow. Like many salmon fishermen in the Kenai River, Bishop had no motor on his boat. He simply paddled into the current and let the boat drift along as he stalked the big king salmon. The fish move up the river in the summer to spawn and die after four years or so in the Pacific Ocean. The obsession to reproduce has drawn them thousands of miles to the trickle of water where they were hatched. They move up the Kenai with their noses close to the ground and a morsel in their faces is enticement enough to attract a strike from some of these big kings.

Using stiff 7-foot rods and Titan reels with 30-pound test monofilament line, Bishop tied on Spin-N-Glo lures above a big hook that he draped with fresh salmon eggs. They're the most popular attractor for salmon on the Kenai. Then we dropped our hooks over the side after the guide tied on jet planers to keep the bright-colored lure and hook near the bottom.

Our lines played out 50 feet behind the boat. We tightened the drags and held on expectantly.

"You've got a strike," Bishop hollered to Darlene. She reeled in a nice rainbow trout that we admired and released. A few minutes later she caught an even larger rainbow, and then a Dolly Varden, another Alaskan species that thrives in the pure water of many of these west coast rivers. Meantime, I hadn't had a bite, and it was about 1 p.m.

Bishop rowed the little skiff out into the middle of the river and anchored. He was tired by now. This would give him a chance to rest a little, and maybe I could get a strike in the deeper water.

Moments later, all my dreams materialized. There was the familiar tap-tap on the rodtip. It was the tell-tale vibration indicating that something was fiddling with my bait. I yanked the rodtip overhead quickly, wound down and jerked again. That ought to set the hook. It was the technique I had been taught years ago, and what worked in Minnesota would surely work in the Kenai.

Like a runaway freight train, the fish headed downriver with my drag grudgingly giving out line. Bishop pulled anchor and paddled frantically, trying to keep up with the mad rush of action.

We were able to keep up with the fish for about an hour. Then it turned upstream and headed for a small island. Rocks jutted up along the shoreline, and my quarry succeeded in wrapping the line around one of the half-submerged boulders. It looked as though I had lost the struggle. Bishop paddled as hard as he could toward the hangup. Then he yelled to three people fishing in a johnboat not far away. He needed assistance, he told them, and he would appreciate their help. The guide graciously put his agreeable clients out on the island, and my wife Darlene stepped out with them. Now it was left to me and the two guides to challenge this fish. I felt optimistic as we got into the 16-foot johnboat with a 35-horsepower Evinrude outboard.

We raced upstream to the rock that my fish had tied out on and managed to untangle the line. The fish, sensing its freedom, took off upstream. We were able to keep up with its flight now and I never let the salmon forget I was challenging it with a rod and reel. I bowed and reeled repeatedly, always keeping the line taut and applying enough tension to tire the critter—or so I thought.

It was some three hours after the hangup when we got our first look at the tenacious creature. The salmon rolled on the surface

long enough for all of us to get a fairly good peep. I was stunned. It was the biggest fish I had ever seen on a line. Both of the veteran guides were also amazed at the bulk of the monster I had hooked. It was a giant.

"That king is as big as the world record 97-pounder hanging in Les Anderson's Ford dealership in Soldotna or I'll eat my hat," Bishop screamed.

Word that a 100-pound salmon and a new world record might be reeled in spread quickly up and down the narrow river. Interested onlookers gathered along the shoreline, shouting encouragement and advice. But I had two experienced guides in the boat. If the tackle held, surely we would eventually get this lunker to the gunnels. I had confidence, even though I had no salmon-fishing experience.

Another guide observed our struggle for a few minutes and agreed to go to the island to pick up the two clients, Darlene and the drift boat we had left there when we untangled the line from around the rock. That removed one worry from our minds.

At 5 p.m. another guide with a 20-foot boat and big outboard offered to take us aboard, allowing the captain of the 16-footer to reload his clients and go back to fishing. I stepped into the bigger boat and Darlene joined me with a bag of hamburgers. I realized then that I hadn't eaten all day, hadn't even thought of it. The challenge of the king had taken my hunger away. But the fragrance of hamburgers and onions proved more than I could resist and I relinquished my rod and reel temporarily to the captain and Darlene. The nourishment and rest were welcome but I was determined to land this fish myself, not with alternating turns on the rod. I gulped down the sandwiches and soft drink and took my rod back in record time.

News of the big salmon hookup had spread and media people motioned to the captain of the 20-foot boat that they wanted to come aboard. He took a cameraman aboard who was anxious to get a first-hand story and pictures of what promised to be a record fish. The bigger boat, even with five people aboard, was roomy enough for us to maneuver and fight the salmon. The king had moved almost five miles downriver at one point, but was now staying nearly still in the same 150-yard stretch of midstream water.

Alaskan summer days last about 20 hours and we were able to get another glimpse of our quarry at 10:30 p.m. when the king

One For The King

again arched on the surface. Shoreline onlookers oohed and aahed along with those of us in the boat who thrilled to the second sighting as first dusk settled over the Kenai. Seeing the salmon renewed my energy and determination to hang on.

Then darkness fell. The kibitzers from shore went home to bed. We stood guard on the silent water, hoping that somehow we would get this monster in the boat. Strangely enough, I wasn't tired, at least not consciously. The challenge of landing this big fish kept my adrenalin flowing.

Throughout the night the two guides plotted strategy for landing the salmon. The king lolled on the bottom of the river, too heavy for me to drag to the surface with 30-pound test line. We had to wait until the fish tired and came up so we could net it.

The plan was to make the salmon move more and tire itself out. The water was relatively shallow. The guides would simply poke at the king with a paddle every time it stopped moving, hoping to make it rush off and use up what stamina it had left. The salmon held to the bottom the rest of the night.

We poked the king with a paddle all the next day. The salmon remained within its 150-yard territory, never getting in a hurry, never using up much energy. Meanwhile, the guides and I used up plenty of energy. The fish was outsmarting us.

Just before dusk on the second day, around 10 p.m., the king decided to move upstream toward the shoreline. The guides flashed lights into the water in an attempt to drive the fish toward shore, because the salmon was only a step or two from the bank in two feet of water. The lights and our proximity to shore brought dozens of onlookers to the spot, anxious to see this final bout with the record-promising king. But when the cameraman's brighter lights were focused on the water, the big fish spooked and headed back toward the open river.

At 1 a.m., 37 hours after the initial hookup, the salmon wedged itself against the bank with the boat almost directly overhead. The water was no more than two feet deep. Success seemed within easy reach. I reeled down until my rodtip was in the water, thumbed the reel, and yanked as hard as I dared without breaking the line. My line must have been pretty well nicked after all those hours of being pulled and sawed over the river rocks. My rod bent, and the salmon's tail fanned the surface while its head stayed down, straining to work free.

Guide Bishop grabbed a huge landing net with a 4-foot diameter mouth. He scooped up the big lunker, enveloping two-thirds of the giant in the net. It was the moment of truth.

As the boat eased away from the bank with the king nearly engulfed in the net, the Spin 'N Glow lure popped out of the fish's mouth. The king surged with more power than it had shown since the original hookup. Somehow, unbelievably, the salmon spun around and was gone in a silver flash. I watched helplessly as my adversary for 37 hours splashed back into the shallow water and headed for the middle of the fast-flowing Kenai River. I had lost a battle that rivaled the one in Hemingway's book, *The Old Man And The Sea.*

I am sure that salmon was gloating as it again headed upstream toward its childhood home. The king was gone, and so were our spirits, energy and the dream of weighing in a world record.

"My heart stopped," said the downcast Bishop. "I almost jumped in after it. But I knew that would do no good. I kept praying, but I guess it was just not meant to be."

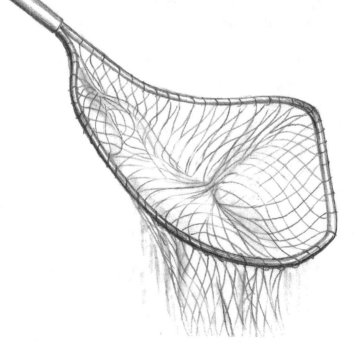

I also had that "we lost everything" attitude as we continued our Alaskan fishing vacation without further action.

Yet, there was a tinge of success even in that losing 37-hour effort. We had enjoyed the privilege of tangling with a great king salmon in a prolific river with beauty all around us. We used the best expertise available, pitting that against the wily tactics and strength of a giant fish determined not to succumb. That fish had evaded Pacific predators and salmon-cannery netters, and confronted many other obstacles in its thousands of miles of ocean journey to get to the Kenai. Out-fighting this latest threat to its objective was just another couple of days in its harried life. I was chagrined at losing the king at the last minute, but perhaps predestination did play a hand.

Darlene and I are sitting out this season. But, the Lord willing, we will be back on the Kenai River next year. We'll be out there drifting a Spin'N Glow with salmon eggs on a big hook, hoping to entice another giant king to strike.

I would relish a chance to struggle another 37 hours with a fish of unparalleled determination and unusual strength. While I may never again have a chance to land a world record, I'll be trying hard when we return to the Kenai River.

Can lightning strike twice?

5

Over The Edge
In A Belly Boat

by Bill Vanderford

Sometimes you escape death's clutches by the narrowest of margins. That's what happened to me on an unforgettable trout-fishing trek on a fast, rocky, mountain river. It happened 10 years ago when Bill Lamont and I decided to fish for trout from belly boats on the jungle-like Chattooga on the northwest Georgia-South Carolina border. A belly boat is a large inner tube that has a canvas floor with holes in it for your legs, sort of like a baby's walker.

I left my car 20 miles downstream and we drove Lamont's back to the access point to start our trout-fishing adventure. It turned out to be much more exciting than we had anticipated.

We each climbed into a belly boat and started floating down the Chattooga about mid-morning on a pretty spring day. You couldn't fish in a conventional boat on this stretch of the river. It was full of fast white-water rapids and rocks. Most of the river was shallow, and we concluded that a belly boat was the best way to fish it.

We had listened to many hair-raising tales of anglers' fights with big rainbow and brown trout in this desolate stretch of water before deciding to make the excursion. With a lightweight flyrod, a few spare flies and jigs, and a creel in case we decided to bring some of our catch home, we were all laughs as the long trek began.

The fishing quickly lived up to our expectations. Nice-size trout were hungry and anxious to strike. The river is fairly narrow in most spots, so I fished one side and Lamont the other. We were close enough to each other to talk back and forth, and we continually bragged on each other's expertise and catch.

Both of us put a few trophy-size rainbows in our creels. They were certainly bragging size back home, and mighty pretty to look at. We looked forward to making a tasty meal of them at day's end. The river and its surrounding scenery was so picturesque that we decided we agreed with the old sage who declared that trout are only caught in beautiful places.

"I bet you never saw anything like this in Scotland," I yelled to Lamont, a native of Glasgow who had moved to Atlanta, Georgia, several years before. "These cliffs on both sides of the river are 60 feet tall and solid rock. This little section of America has barely changed since Columbus came over." The forests at the top of the cliffs stretched for miles. There wasn't a house or highway closer than 20 miles.

"We have some pretty mountain streams in Scotland, and some fine brown trout too," the fun-loving Scotsman retorted. "But I admit this is a gorgeous river to fish. We'll probably be telling our grandchildren about this float trip." Little did he know how prophetic that statement would turn out to be.

The current quickened and the water got noisier as it dashed over and around rocks. There were tiny whirlpools and eddies behind the bigger boulders, great spots in which to flip a fly. Trout stalked insects in the calm little pools where the floating bugs circled lazily a round or two before being caught up in the rapids and rushed downstream.

We each found a productive pool and concentrated on catching fish. I didn't notice Lamont was lagging several hundred yards behind me until it was too late.

Then it happened so fast that I barely had time to yell for help. My belly boat drifted around a curve, and I was thrown right into a killer rapid. The current was so swift that my kicking and paddling had no effect. The super-fast water was something I had not counted on; I was at its mercy.

Lamont heard me holler and watched as I bounced over the surface like a fishing cork in a tailrace. I was hanging on to my fishing tackle for dear life. My trout in the creel were experiencing a roller coaster ride.

Then it dawned on me—that louder noise I had heard several minutes before I rounded the curve wasn't just water rushing

Over The Edge In A Belly Boat

down this rapid. There was a steep waterfall less than a football field away. I looked downstream at the top of the falls. It appeared as though the water dropped off the edge of the horizon. Bobbing and swirling ever closer to the falls I fought desperately to hang on to a rock and escape being swept over the tumbling water.

I was in the clutches of the devil. If I could have fought out of the belly boat I may have been able to struggle to shore. But the holes in the canvas were just large enough for my legs. There was no escape. Like a lifeless log, I rolled over and was pulled under in a relentless race toward the roaring waterfall.

Yelling at the top of my voice, I approached the precipice, catching a fleeting glance of Lamont far behind as he struggled to get out of the current. Panic squeezed my heart as I tumbled through the cascading water, over the rocky ledge, and fell 50 feet straight down.

As I dropped through the falls head first and waited what seemed like an eternity to hit the bottom I thought back over my years on earth. It seemed so ironic that I was going to be killed on these rocks after I had defied death for 10 years in Europe as a racecar driver. There, every race could have ended my life, as it had the lives of many of my racing friends. But I came through strong and healthy. Now I would be broken to bits at the bottom of a waterfall while trying to catch another rainbow trout. It was a strange way to end it all.

Then I hit bottom. I plunged into deep water for a moment, then popped to the surface. There were no rocks at the bottom of the cliff where I landed. Spitting and sputtering, my flyrod gone and my creel of trout torn loose, I looked around. The current was still strong and spinning me around. Desperately, I clung to a protruding rock and worked a little closer to the shore. I happily grasped an overhanging limb from a bush that grew out of the rocky cliff.

I learned later that a much higher waterfall was only a quarter mile farther downstream, and all of it poured out on the rocks below. I could not have survived that fall. I hung on to my bush for dear life.

Minutes later Lamont worked down the cliff and pulled me up on a narrow ledge. While our position was still precarious we now had a chance to survive. I had lived through the 50-foot fall, and that was a miracle.

Over The Edge In A Belly Boat   41

"Man, all I thought about when I saw you go over the falls was how on earth was I ever going to get your body out of this river," Lamont told me later. "I don't know whether it could have been done or not. It surely is great to know I don't have to face that problem." He looked at me with tears in his Scottish eyes.

While I had survived the plunge, our troubles were not over. We had the tall, rocky cliffs to climb before we could get back to safety. There were no gentle riverbanks, only sheer cliffs. Halfway up I slipped on a tiny ledge and was again in trouble. I would have fallen to my death or a terrible injury on the rocks below, but Lamont grabbed my belt and held on until I got my footing.

I don't think I have ever said "thank you" with such heart-felt emotion as I did right then. Without Lamont's help I wouldn't have left the Chattooga alive.

We made it back to my car and a few hours later we were home in Lawrenceville. It has since crossed my mind that I could probably be content just making a living as a guide on Lake Lanier and writing the outdoor news for the Guinett Daily News. It's a much safer life than flying headlong down a waterfall in an inner tube.

6

Riding An Ice Floe

by Roger Hoyle

Gazing out my second-floor window onto Saginaw Bay on Lake Huron near Linwood, Michigan, I suddenly realized that the group of fishermen a quarter of a mile away were moving slowly out to sea on a giant slab of ice that had broken loose. A big chasm already separated the floe from land, and those anglers out there would soon be at the mercy of the strong wind and bone-chilling cold that was sweeping over the bay that morning, January 20, 1989.

Two or three of the fishermen on the ice were frantically waving and shouting as they ran around near the gap in the ice floe. It was constantly widening, and already much too wide for even good swimmers, particularly in such freezing conditions. Their yells attracted the attention of others on the runaway slab.

But several of the 18 men and two young boys on the maverick ice floe were not even aware that they were floating away. The sharp cracking noise that shattered the stillness along the shoreline when the ice broke loose had not alerted the anglers who were enjoying the winter day catching walleyes and perch through the ice holes. They were oblivious to the danger that stalked them. I had to do something.

Similar ice floe break-offs occur in Lake Huron and other Great Lakes regularly during the winter, and many fishermen have drowned, or died of hypothermia. The real danger comes when the floating ice breaks up in the open water. This often occurs in cold, windy weather. Death comes quickly after that.

Riding An Ice Floe

Breakaways occur when the water level changes drastically because of strong winds that push waves across the long expanses of water in the same direction for prolonged periods. This raises the water level, and puts incredible strain on the ice, making it break and float. Once it detaches from the shoreline it may float slowly into the vast, sea-like waters of Lake Huron. The floes often carry unsuspecting fishermen who are so absorbed with watching a bobber in a hole in the ice that they are at first ignorant of their situation. By the time many anglers realize they are afloat, they may be too far from shore to make themselves seen or heard. At that point, they are helpless and lost unless the U.S. Coast Guard or other rescuers discover the trapped ice fishermen and carry them ashore.

I called the Coast Guard immediately, and then rushed down the steps to my boat. I operate Hoyle's Marina on Saginaw Bay, having built it in 1972, and my 14-foot, flat-bottomed boat is always near the water in case just such an emergency arises.

"Come a runnin'," I yelled to my nephew who was helping me at the marina. It took only a few seconds to launch the little boat and head toward the ice floe.

Now a 14-foot boat in big, troubled water like we had in the bay that morning is not an ideal rescue vessel. White caps polka-dotted the surface, and it was obvious that getting to the stranded fishermen would not be without danger. Waves began breaking over the bow even before we reached the floe, and our ponchos glistened as the icy water froze.

By that time, most of the fishermen had discovered they were afloat, and realized the danger. They moved to the edge of the ice as I maneuvered the little craft next to the floe.

"Three of you get in the boat quickly," I hollered. "I'll run in with those, and be back as fast as I can." The anglers were at least half of a mile from shore at that point.

The two young boys and one adult jumped in the boat and I quickly turned it around and headed toward the marina. I soon realized that loading five people in such a small skiff was a mistake. We were heavy in the water and every wave drenched us. Hypothermia would certainly become a danger if we were delayed out here very long.

I reached the dock, unloaded the scared fishermen, and headed back to the floe. All the time the massive chunk of white

Riding An Ice Floe

ice was moving farther and farther from shore. Shivering in the cold and wet to the skin, we made it back to the ice. Three fishermen stepped toward the boat, but I waved one of them off. We would carry only two at a time. Maybe the waves wouldn't break over the bow so much.

I knew it was going to be a long ordeal rescuing just two passengers each trip, and the distance was increasing all the time. There were 15 people left on the floe, but we couldn't chance being swamped in this rough water.

I began talking again with the Coast Guard from my hand-held radio. They had dispatched helicopters from Detroit and Traverse City, and they were in the area. I told them that it was going to be difficult for us to rescue all the fishermen before the floe got too far away. We could use some assistance.

Unfortunately, they had received reports that a group of fishermen two miles down the shore had also been caught in the ice break-off, and were in even greater danger because their flow was breaking up. They left me to continue the rescue while they searched for the anglers in the water.

As it turned out, the report they received was false. They found no one, but continued their search as we made trip after trip in worsening conditions hauling the stranded ice fishermen to shore.

Then, the wind changed. Instead of pushing the floe farther and farther away from land, the wind moved the floe parallel to the beach. It was not as rough inside the bay, and the distance we had to run on each trip was reduced. That wind change was a real godsend; I'm certain it saved the lives of several of the fishermen.

There were a few anglers with expensive, gasoline-powered ice augers who were reluctant to abandon their equipment. One pair even had a three-wheeler on the ice, and all had tackle boxes, rods, reels and other equipment. They came to the boat with the tackle, but I made them leave it on the ice. It was tough enough to get to shore with the people in the boat. We could not save their equipment unless by chance the floe headed for the shoreline. In that unlikely case (though it has happened in the past) the fishermen could walk back on the floe and retrieve their gear.

Coast Guard helicopters gave up their search after it was determined the report was made in error, and headed back to help.

"We'll get the last three," said the radio operator as I headed back to the marina with my last two fishermen.

"That's fine with me," I radioed back as I watched them setting the bird down softly on the ice. They loaded the last three of the stranded men and I breathed a little easier.

There was an impromptu reunion at the marina as the last angler escaped the runaway ice floe.

By the time we were all safe and sound we learned that a severe offshore wind had developed that surely would have broken up the big ice floe, had the wind not brought it alongside the beach. Several of those anglers might have been dumped in the freezing water because rough wave action makes ice floes break up quickly into much smaller pieces. Rescue at that point with my little boat, or even with the helicopters might have been impossible.

Thinking back to that day, you can't really find fault with the fishermen caught on that floe. Many had fished this bay for years. They fished on what appeared to them to be safe ice. It just happened that a stronger than normal wind made larger than normal waves, and this effectively separated the ice from the beach. They were trapped by a weird quirk of nature. It has happened before on

Saginaw Bay, but it is always a surprise.

Two of the men on the ice that memorable January morning were Dale Johnson of Bay City and Jack Doughtery of Clarkson. Veteran ice fishermen, they shrugged off the experience as just another day in the life of ice-fishing enthusiasts.

More thankful for the rescue was Dale Bergey, of Sanford. He was out there with his two young sons. He shudders when he thinks of how the wind could have carried them into the big water, broken the ice pack and snuffed out their lives.

I'm glad the episode had a happy ending. No one suffered more than a bad cold, and some uncomfortable hours. Some equipment had to be abandoned, but that is inconsequential compared to loss of life. I'm just glad I had a chance to help in a rescue when there was no other assistance nearby. I saw the breakaway ice at just the right time to do something about it.

I've been thinking about getting a bigger, faster boat just in case there's another ice break-off and no one else around to haul in the stranded. We'll see.

7

Snakebite By Proxy

by Calvin A. Stone

S quirming and groaning as he lay in his tent deep in the Big Cypress Swamp area of the Florida Everglades, Ralph Hamilton, one of the toughest old swamp rats I have ever known, was uncharacteristically complaining.

I had seen this old man, who called his humble home in the Big Cypress "Camp Misery," working with a broken arm, broken hands and once hobbling about with a homemade truss outside his overalls that held a bad scrotum rupture in place. He was tough by every yardstick, and to see him taking on like he was on that hot summer morning meant he was in serious trouble.

His camp was not far from mine, and I frequently visited with him to see if he was all right. This particular day, however, I walked into his camp almost by accident. I wanted some panfish for lunch and I decided to fish for bluegills along the shoreline of a creek near Hamilton's camp.

I had a half-dozen nice panfish on a stringer before I got near Hamilton's old camp. The big bream apparently were hungry that morning, and they dived on every small grasshopper bait I put on my hook. I was alone in the swamp at my camp at the time and didn't need that many fish for my noon meal. I knew my old swamp buddy liked fried bream better than Western steak and would appreciate me sharing my catch. I made a slight detour to get to his tent.

A horrible stench hit me when I opened the flap on his tent and walked in. But there was almost always a bad smell in Ralph's place. He was not the best housekeeper. Often his old overalls looked like they would stand alone from the grease and grime covering them. But I did know he washed them from time to time. I had seen him take them off, go to a pond not far from his tent, and scrub them with his hands and homemade soap until they looked reasonably clean. He would then hang them on a cypress limb in the sun until they were dry enough to wear again.

Today he wasn't in any shape to wash anything. He was the sickest I had ever seen him. It can be fatal to be really sick deep in the Big Cypress Swamp alone when you have no way of getting out by yourself.

"What's your trouble, Ralph?" I inquired.

"I really don't know what the trouble is. I know my leg is hurting like crazy. I can hardly stand the pain, and I've been running a high fever for two or three days. I kept hoping you would come by, because I can't get out to catch me a mess of fish or do anything until I get better," Hamilton groaned.

"I can take care of that mess of fish for you. I have enough here to feed us both. That's why I came by. But right now I have got to see that leg. It's so dark in here, let's go outside," I suggested.

With my help, he hobbled out of the old tent, and I lifted him into an ancient hemp hammock that hung between two giant pines in his front yard.

I rolled up his overalls, and saw one of the worst looking legs I ever saw on any man. It was swollen from the ankle to the knee. It was fit to burst and parts of it were almost black. The only sign of an injury was a fairly deep scratch, four or five inches long on the calf of his leg. Hamilton had wrapped a dirty piece of an old denim shirt around the scratch and blood had oozed through it.

"How did you get that scratch?" I asked. "It looks like it is several days old."

"I was working on that swamp buggy you helped me design. I got over-balanced when I was welding on the top and fell plumb off the thing. My leg dragged across the unfinished metal seat I was fastening to the chassis. It was just a scratch and didn't even hurt. That's not what has me so sick," Ralph said emphatically.

I had to agree with that assumption. The scratch wouldn't have caused this kind of swelling and discoloration. At least, that would not be the usual.

Having lived in this desolate swamp much of my life, I had

Complete Angler's Library

seen many snakebites from rattlers and cottonmouth moccasins. The swollen, blackened leg with the swelling starting at the ankle and moving up was symptomatic of a moccasin bite. But I looked the leg over well. There were no tell-tale fang marks of a bite from a poisonous viper.

"Mr. Hamilton, you sure look like a man suffering from a poisonous snakebite, but I can't find any sign of a bite."

"I'd know if I was bit by a snake, wouldn't I? Ain't no snake smart enough to bite me, and me not even know about it. I've been bit before. It stings pretty bad when they sink those old crooked fangs in your leg. I sure ain't been bit by no snake this time," Hamilton insisted.

But the leg looked so much like it was swollen from snake venom that I kept looking and talking. The skin was almost tight enough to break, and even a little pressure brought more groans of discomfort from the old swamper.

Hamilton was noted for always wearing his boots. He knew this gave him some protection from the moccasins that were plentiful around all the streams and water holes in Big Cypress Swamp. His waist-high boots were a kind of Hamilton trademark. He seldom went walking through any part of this wild, watery wilderness without wearing them.

"Mr. Hamilton, have you been anywhere around here without those boots on?" I pursued my snake-bite diagnosis.

"Yeah, last Saturday I was fishing an old slough up the branch there and I wanted to get on the other bank. It was so deep that the water came right up under my arm pits. Wasn't no use wearing hip boots in a slough that deep. So, I pulled them off and left them on the bank until I came back across," Hamilton said.

"Did you maybe get bit under the water while you were crossing the slough?" I asked, hoping to solve the mystery.

"Naw, but there was a big old cottonmouth on the bank when I got there. He took to the water to get away. I busted him across the back with my fishing pole two or three times, and killed him before I started across. He sunk out there in the slough. He couldn't have bit me. He was dead."

Hamilton told his story while gently rubbing his aching ankle. "But that was one mad moccasin. He struck my pole several times and that old cotton-white mouth looked mighty menacing. I smashed his head good after I broke his back."

Now the secret was unlocked.

"The water wasn't moving much where you killed the snake, was it? And you had that fresh cut on your leg. You went in there immediately after that moccasin had struck your pole. He spewed out his venom when he struck, and it was in the water where you crossed the slough. It went right in that cut on your calf. Mr. Hamilton, you have been snakebit without knowing it just as surely as if those fangs had stuck in your leg," I versed the old codger on his plight.

He had beaten the snake's head to pieces, and that had released more venom from the poison bags in the snake's cheeks.

"You have been snakebit by proxy," I said with a smile. "But now that we know what the trouble is, I have to get you to a doctor. That bite could cause you even greater trouble." I knew certain snakebites could be fatal if left unattended, and a cottonmouth's was one.

I went after my swamp buggy with the tall wheels and we sloshed through the marshes and quicksand to the highway where I had left my car closer to civilization at a friend's house. Four hours later, we walked into the nearest doctor's office in the little hamlet of Immokalee. It had been a long, uncomfortable ride from Mr. Hamilton's appropriately-named Camp Misery to the little town on the outer fringe of the desolate Everglades.

The doctor complimented me on my diagnosis and confirmed the snakebite. He cleaned out the infected scratch, and gave the victim some medication. The water had diluted the venom enough that Mr. Hamilton would recover, but he would still have several days of pain and soreness. He didn't get the medical attention a bit too soon.

A week later, he was back working on his new swamp buggy. Ever after, Hamilton liked to tell about the time he was bitten by proxy by a cottonmouth moccasin in his favorite fishing slough a short distance from Camp Misery. He also vowed that henceforth he would stay out of the water where he killed a moccasin, at least until the venom had a chance to disperse. As it turned out, snakebite by proxy didn't hurt any less than the real thing.

8

Last Cast . . . .

by W. Horace Carter

Charles Arnette snatched an unopened bloom from a spatterdock lily in Lake Lochloosa. The water held a vast array of greenery that glistened in the morning rain. Charles looked at the lily bulb a moment, then tied it on his fishing line three feet above a fluttering, live shiner. He wondered whether this would be his last fishing trip. Perhaps. But if so, he would make the most of it. He had vowed to catch one more 10-pound bass before his time ran out.

While most live-bait bass anglers used various colorful plastic bobbers, Charles was sure that a simple natural float would be least obnoxious to a trophy bass in the lilies. A lily-bulb bobber was something the fish saw every day in their territory. It was not manmade, and shouldn't tip off the big bass that something unusual was going on beneath it.

With his humble Stumpbumper boat anchored fore and aft in the six-foot deep, warm tannic water, Charles flipped his bait within arm's length of the lily line. It fluttered crazily out of sight in a bathtub-size hole in the cover, a big-bass hideout. The bulb danced on the surface as the impaled live bait cavorted below.

It was time for patience and watchfulness. For Charles Arnette, it was a precious time to think.

The fourth of seven children born at New Smyrna Beach, Florida, 35 years before, Arnette came from a family of outdoorsmen. His grandfather and father lived off the land and the water as hunters and fishermen, often feasting on giant sea turtles and their eggs as a major treat from nature.

The most common foods on their table were venison, rabbit, squirrel, turkey and 'possum from the swamplands; crabs, shrimp, fish, frogs and alligator tail from the water. Charles remembered the morning he was fishing out here on Lochloosa alone with a cane pole when he hooked something big. For half an hour he fought a powerful demon, eventually dragging a mossy-back old freshwater turtle to the surface. Back at the Cross Creek Fishing Camp, it weighed in at 42 pounds, a real reptile monster. The battle with the turtle made him think of the days of his youth, and the now-endangered sea turtles.

He recalled the dozens of times when tourist anglers needed help in finding the bedding bluegills and shellcrackers, always plentiful at Cross Creek in the spring and summer. Because he fished nearly every day, he knew where the spawning areas were and often located the honey holes that might elude a novice. He always delighted in being a little help to people not as versed in fishing and hunting as he was. After all, he cut his teeth on a gun-shell and a fishing reel handle.

Arnette's mind drifted to some of the tragedies of his life. Both he and his mother had almost died when he was born. The difficult childbirth left him weak and sickly for years. As a boy, he developed a unique kidney ailment that kept him in the hospital for months, often on the brink of death. Gradually, he overcame the handicap, and became a Phi Beta Kappa in wilderness knowledge. His hunting-fishing family taught him volumes by the time he was 12. He was knowledgeable enough to hunt and fish alone even at that early age.

Then came another debacle. When he was 16, he went turkey hunting with a high school chum. They separated in the woods. Charles called a big gobbler into his gunsight and shot him. He yelled for his hunting partner, but could not raise him. He thought he might see his buddy if he climbed up a tall steel tower that supported several high-powered electric lines. He scaled the ladder and looked in every direction for his buddy. He was nowhere in sight. A little frustrated, Charles carelessly fired his shotgun into the air from up on the tower, hoping that the blast would bring his hunting companion running. Instead, the kick from the gunshot rammed the barrel against one of the high-voltage wires. In a freak accident, Charles had given himself a tremendous shock.

He tumbled to the ground unconscious. He was barely alive when rescuers carried him into the hospital hours later. When he finally regained consciousness, he throbbed from head to foot, more than half of his body had suffered severe third-degree burns. He was a pitiful sight when his family arrived.

He underwent dozens of surgical procedures during the next nine months. Every Monday morning meant more surgery and unbelievable suffering as doctors tried to restore his body. He had completely lost the use of his left arm, and being a left-hander, he had to learn to make his right arm the stronger. The left one had almost withered away. Determination would make him whole again.

While suffering far beyond the endurance levels of most young men, Arnette refused to take morphine, the leading painkiller of the time. He didn't want to be dependent upon any kind of drugs. He just gritted his teeth and withstood the constant pain month after month, even when the rotting skin and muscle smelled so badly that he had to spray his body and bed several times a day to reduce the sickening odor that filled his hospital room.

Finally, the operations over and his body almost a skeleton, he was sent home. His spirit had never died. In a matter of a few weeks he was back on his feet, fiddling with a rod and reel and a bow and arrow; testing the right arm that now had to be his strength.

He could still aim and shoot, and proved it by quickly killing a trophy-size buck in Georgia, and a long-bearded old turkey gobbler near his Smyrna Beach home. It was time to renew his fishing career, something he had cherished all of his young life. Soon he could cast a lure to a pork and bean can at 60 feet.

He grew up and was almost as physically fit as ever when he moved to Cross Creek in Alachua County, Central Florida, where he had relatives who were outdoors people like he was. Hunting and fishing continued to be his first loves.

At Cross Creek he was a favorite of native and visiting fishermen, often sharing his expertise on the habitat of the 23,000 acres of water in Orange and Lochloosa lakes. Many who could not catch fish came to Charles for help. Often their encounter with him changed their luck overnight.

Then came more disaster. Charles' head began throbbing severely, unmercifully. He became disoriented. He had difficulty getting his legs into his pants, often putting both in the same hole. When he tried to cast a plug, he missed by yards. Something had gone wrong! He checked into the hospital for tests. The results confirmed brain cancer. Surgeons operated and, remarkably, he was fishing happily again only a month later, shaved head and all.

But fate hadn't finished with Charles yet. A smelly, mushroom-like sore suddenly sprouted from his leg. The cancer was not dead. He went back to the hospital and had another operation. He came back home, recuperated, and was fishing again. Charles seemed to override every obstacle.

The tumor quickly returned, this time in his brain again. He went through horrible surgery a third and fourth time. Still, it came back. There was no end to the cancer's resurgence.

No more! Charles had stood all he could, and every operation led to another one as his body shrank and shriveled away. Quietly he thanked the bevy of understanding doctors for all they had done.

"I won't go through another operation," he said. "My time is obviously about over. I have only a few simple requests, and then I'll be ready to meet my Maker. I want to kill one more 10-point buck, and catch one more 10-pound bass, and then I'll be ready to go," he said with tears in his eyes.

A month later, Arnette pulled the bow string on his Fred Bear compound bow, and sent an arrow through the heart of a giant whitetail buck on the Lochloosa Wildlife Refuge. Half of his request was fulfilled.

Today, Charles watched the green spatterdock lily bulb floating in the opening. Suddenly, it whirled in a circle and darted toward the boat and the open water. Pop! It almost left a hole in the water it sank so fast. Calm as usual, Charles raised the rod tip and set the hook with as much gusto as his withered muscles would allow. There was a hookup. He fought the big bass all around the boat, eventually bringing it to boatside. He lipped the lunker, admired it a moment and dropped it into the livewell. It was time to head for home.

Back at the fish camp, the bass weighed 10-pounds, 4-ounces. Charles carefully slipped the bass into the creek and watched it swim away. He tied up his boat at his uncle's canal dock, wound up his line, and carried his rod, reel and tackle box inside the house. He left them in a corner of the den, and walked to his bedroom.

Charles died in his room two days later, suffering horribly to the very end. All his life had been punctuated with misery and pain, yet he seemed to have enjoyed life far more than the healthy people around him. He had cherished every moment of his years. A letter on a table by his bedside made this request:

"Cremate what remains of my old diseased body. It's the one way that I know this cancer will die. I wasn't able to kill it while I was alive, and I don't want it buried in the ground. Burn it to ashes. Then take my ashes on a pretty sunny afternoon and slowly scatter them over Orange and Lochloosa. I loved those lakes, and I want a little part of me to be there forever. Maybe my last 10-pounder will be close by."

Charles Arnette's ashes settled to the bottom of the Cross Creek lakes. At last his suffering was over. But not the memory of him. Tourists still stop by the fish camps and ask about the young man who once helped them catch a mess of fish. His sisters and

brothers had shuddered at his almost constant suffering, yet they smile when thinking of the grin that graced his face when he came home with another stringer of fish or a gobbler across his back. Charles Arnette was happy because he appreciated what he had, and didn't fret over what he didn't. Even in death, he casts a big shadow that brings back refreshing memories of a life beset by turmoil from birth, yet rewarding in a strange sort of way to all who knew him. Most people seek throughout a lifetime for an untenable something called happiness that is always just beyond their grasp. Most never quite catch up with it.

Charles Arnette caught up with it by sharing with others—sharing such natural discoveries as fishing with lily-bulb bobbers on Lake Lochloosa.

9

Lake Nightmare

by Dean DeRosier

Rumors of fantastic walleye catches on Lake Mille Lacs enticed my friend and me to roam farther afield than usual one Labor Day weekend. Usually, we fished closer to our Brainerd, Minnesota, home at Gull Lake. But the urge to catch big walleyes on the mud flats at Mille Lacs proved to be overwhelming.

We hitched our boat trailer to the car, and made the 90-minute drive to central Minnesota's premier walleye honey hole. At 9 a.m. we launched our 14-foot fiberglass speedboat with its 85-horsepower outboard motor at Garrison on the northwest corner of the lake. We headed toward a mud flat area about five miles offshore across a good chop.

We should have taken that chop as a warning that 14-foot speedboats weren't safe on this 132,000-acre, wind-swept lake. Mille Lacs has a reputation for being treacherous. Because it is so shallow, even a light wind can make it very rough. But the fact that a half-million pounds of walleye are harvested there every year was enough to make two healthy 20-year-old outdoorsmen throw caution to the wind.

By the time we reached our selected mud flat, surface fog had reduced visibility so much that we could not make out the shoreline in either direction. But we didn't need the shore in order to catch walleyes, so we tipped our Lindy Rigs with leeches and began drifting broadside to the wind and waves.

After two hours of dragging those baits over the mud flat, we had not caught a walleye or had a nibble. As noon approached we decided to head back to Garrison and enjoy a seafood lunch at the famous Blue Goose Inn.

But the motor wouldn't start. We tried cranking the engine with the battery for an hour, draining it of its charge. After taking off the motor cowling we worked ourselves to near exhaustion pulling on the emergency crank rope. When we stopped to rest I noticed that the boat had a slow leak through the stern. Normally, this wouldn't have been a problem, as the bilge pump would have quickly forced it out. But with the battery dead, the bilge pump was useless. We took turns bailing and cranking the outboard.

We didn't get panicky but continued to joke and josh about our boat problem. Other boats on the horizon appeared as tiny dots. They were too far away to hear our calls for help. I found a brightly-colored piece of chrome in the bottom of the boat and signaled with it, using it like a mirror against the occasional rays of sun that poked through the cumulus clouds. No one got the message, though I signaled for half an hour. I tossed it back on the deck, and told Kevin we might as well start paddling.

We had one paddle and a water ski. With both of us working we figured we could make it back to Garrison by nightfall. It's amazing how tired you can get paddling in the waves and wind with an oar, much less with an awkward water ski. We gave it up after about an hour, hoping to drift into shore eventually. Three hours later darkness began to close in and the wind picked up. We could see the boats, miles away, moving. We waved and yelled frantically to no avail.

In desperation we pulled off our pants, doused them with gasoline, set them on fire and threw them into the air, hoping to attract attention. The blaze fizzled in the water and went out. We poured more gasoline on the water and set it aflame. That produced quite a fire even in the rough waves, but it brought no help. We joked about how we would look, coming home in underwear and life jackets

Breakers three- to four-feet high were now pouring water over the stern regularly. We went back to bailing. The breakers got higher and we were getting exhausted. We decided to take turns bailing so that one of us could rest for a time. But weariness overtook both of us and we began to snooze in the rocking craft.

We were awakened suddenly by water rushing over our backs.

An unusually high wave, sometimes called a "rogue" wave, had enveloped the boat, filling it to the gunnels.

"Jump over the side," Kevin yelled. Without thinking, we both plunged into the water.

Unbelievably, we were still in good spirits and even joked about taking a swim in the middle of the lake at midnight in our underwear.

We were glad we'd donned our life jackets when the waves had picked up—though we knew you could drown despite wearing even a good life jacket, as many fishermen do every year. Our life jackets were old, damaged and torn. It made me wish I had been

more observant of their condition before.

The heavy motor on the stern pulled the back of the boat under water, but there was enough buoyancy to keep a bit of the bow above the surface. We grabbed hold of the bow and hung on. I dived under the floating bow and found the ski rope. Kevin took the line, and tied himself securely to the boat. He grasped the rope, and I held on to him. Still optimistic, we rode that boat bow as though it was a bucking bronco and even laughed about it.

The waves got higher and crashed over our heads as we struggled in the wee hours of the morning. Then there came a ray of hope as the first faint fingers of dawn streaked across the lake. We thought we surely would have drifted in closer to shore during the night. But as the sun rose we were still bobbing in the vast expanse of water with no land in sight.

Discouraged, knowing we could not survive another day in the water with coldness creeping into our bodies, fatigued, hungry and no longer able to joke, I made a decision that is usually fatal. I told Kevin I would swim to shore somehow and get help. I told him to stay tied to the boat. Then I began swimming with the waves, hoping that land was in that direction, and not too far away. The life jacket helped keep me afloat. I dog-paddled, swam on my back and used every stroke I had ever learned to keep going in the same direction. I kept changing strokes so that my muscles wouldn't cramp.

I soon found that while I had started with the waves, they seemed to constantly change direction. I would have them at my back for awhile, and then they would hit me in the face as I tried desperately to go in a straight line. While I didn't know how miraculous my decision was to swim in that direction, I was grateful later. I had chosen a direction only five miles off the shoreline. Had I gone any other direction, it would have been an impossible 15-mile swim. That decision now seems divine.

Hours passed. I was so tired I could barely put one hand in front of the other. The life jacket was soaked and heavy now and would no longer keep my face above the surface. I sank time after time, but the little bit of buoyancy left in the jacket, plus my struggling feet and hands, kept me from drowning.

The severity of my situation finally hit me. I had been on the lake more than 24 hours, the last 19 desperately trying to stay alive. I decided to swim myself to death. That would be better than drowning, I reasoned. I began paddling and kicking as fast as I could. I supposed that Kevin was already dead. I thought about my wife, Joann, and our two daughters. Little Jennifer was only one month old. She wouldn't even remember me. But maybe my three-year-old, Tabatha, would think of me sometimes.

Finally, I started to sink. My legs felt as heavy as logs. I gave one last, weak kick and my foot struck something. It was the bottom! I tried to stand up. But I immediately fell back into the surf, my legs too weak to support my weight. I had to crawl out of the waves.

After a few minutes' rest, during which I thanked God I'd made it to shore, I staggered up the beach on rubbery legs in my underwear and tattered life jacket. My eyes focused on an endless flight of stairs up a steep hill to a house above. Was this the staircase to heaven? I could never make it to the top. All those dark hours clinging to our swamped boat, and the miles of torturous swimming in rough water and strong wind, had all but sapped me of my senses. Exhaustion gripped my mind, and every muscle ached, weak and almost useless.

The next thing I remember is staring into the faces of two well-

dressed men as I lay on a couch. They must have helped me make it up those impossible stairs. Then I stammered that my fishing friend was still out there in the lake hanging onto a boat. He needed help. Indeed, he might be drowned by now. And surely if he were still alive, he would be saddened at the thought of having to return to Brainerd and tell my wife and daughters of my demise in Lake Mille Lacs.

The rescue unit arrived, and a search boat was dispatched. In a few minutes they found Kevin still tied to the bow of the boat. He was overjoyed to be alive, and elated to learn that I had made it to shore.

I was treated in the local hospital for hypothermia and released eight hours later. Kevin remained in the hospital overnight, as his body temperature had dropped to 88 degrees and his hypothermic condition was serious. But the next day he came home with no lasting physical damage.

Our families back in Brainerd had spent a sleepless, nervous night. When we failed to return around dark as was our usual custom, they believed we had been in a car wreck. They waited throughout the night by the phone expecting to get a message of an accident that never came.

The ordeal had been so traumatic that Kevin doesn't like to talk about it. He still lives and fishes in Brainerd. Memories of that disastrous time on Mille Lacs, however, are unmentionable.

Several times I have driven back to Lake Mille Lacs and looked out at the vast expanse of water. But I don't fish that lake anymore.

10

Imprisoned By A Cottonmouth

by W. Horace Carter

R edwing blackbirds hung on the sawgrass, and fussed with the boattail grackles that hopped from one flat spatterdock lily to another. An osprey squawked over-head, and dived for shad around the hydrilla of Orange Lake's shoreline. A cawing crow winged over the boat and settled in a cypress hammock. A lone limpkin pecked at insects in the maidencane.

A few scattered splashes disrupted the calm water as yearling largemouth bass and feeding crappies hustled after the gambusia minnows schooled along the lily line. A stoic great blue heron and a smaller egret posed motionless, like long-necked statues, watch-ing ever-so-intensely for a meal of small fish. The surface of the lake was as peaceful as a plate glass window. It was a beautiful fall Florida morning with all of God's artistry on display. Indeed, it was a day to remember.

Lindy Evans teaches youngsters how to fish in a Valdosta, Georgia, Middle School, and at Valdosta State College. He had driven down to Cross Creek where I live, hoping we could catch a few bluegills and shellcrackers that were bedding in the open water a few yards from the hydrilla line. We had shoved off from the Cross Creek Fish Camp at about 7:30 in the morning.

Soon we anchored in six feet of water and we baited No. 10 hooks with live grass shrimp. We used light lines with no cork and no lead on 10-foot fiberglass poles. A few minutes after dropping the hooks in the water, we began pulling huge copperhead bream (known as bluegills in most parts of the country) over the gunnels every few minutes. It kept us rather busy, but not too occupied to see the mean head and eyes of a cottonmouth moccasin that was swimming toward the boat from the shoreline cover. He seemed to be on a charted course for our bass boat, but a few splashes with a heavy paddle convinced the poisonous reptile to submerge. We expected that noisy attack against the critter to end the disruption of our successful morning. How wrong we were!

Minutes later, the same sneaky, snake eyes popped up on the starboard side. Again the moccasin headed straight for the boat, as if he were on a mission. It wasn't until sometime later that we realized he had smelled our bream in the livewell and wanted us to share with him. For the second time, we threatened the moccasin with the heavy plastic paddle, and he dived again when we splashed water in his face.

We fished in peace for another hour. Lindy once had three big bream in the boat at once and I was busy putting his fish in the stern livewell. I occupied the pedestal seat in the rear of the boat, and he was having most of the fun in the bow. But I was guiding him, and didn't mind being beaten if this was a contest for the longest stringer.

"Catch one more and we'll head home," I told him. "It's 11 o'clock and getting too hot for me."

He acknowledged the remark, and immediately pulled in a nice shellcracker, unhooked the fish and tossed it on the deck at my feet so I could reach it. I picked up the titty bream (so called because they are so large you have to hold them against your chest to get them off the hook), opened the livewell lid, and dropped the fish in the water. I took one look and slammed the lid, barely believing my eyes. Striking short of my hand by less than four inches, a mad cottonmouth moccasin struggled and squirmed from under the livewell seat.

"That cottonmouth is in the livewell with the fish!" I yelled. "He almost bit me, and would have if I hadn't moved like greased lightning!"

"You must be kidding," Lindy replied.

"You take a look," I said, standing up and holding down the livewell lid. Then I opened it no more than an inch or two for Lindy when that ugly snake popped his head out the opening and looked me right in the eye. I slammed the lid, and it pinched the snake three or four inches from the head. It made him fighting mad. Almost instantly he squeezed out of the livewell with his white mouth open and poison fangs glistening. He struck the padded lid and his curved teeth locked in the plastic cover. I hit the squirming, struggling snake with the paddle while trying to hold him in the box with the lid. This simply further maddened the

critter. He slid out of the livewell and made a dash for my bare legs. I was wearing loafers and short shorts. Right then I swore I'd never wear shorts again when I was fishing.

Instantly, I was standing with one foot on the console and the other on the storage seat. The mad moccasin was squirming all over the deck where I had stood a second earlier. He was viciously striking everything he could reach. Fortunately, he couldn't quite get to me on the console, and Lindy was high and dry standing on the bow pedestal seat. He had forgotten about fishing. It was apparent that there was no place to run, and that four-foot viper had taken over our boat. He was truly the captain at that moment in time.

I held on to the old, plastic paddle and looked for an opening so I could bash that snake's head in. But he was adroit at squirming around the gas can, the batteries, the tackle box and even my driver's seat in openings so small I couldn't get a clean whack at him. Lindy looked for a weapon to defend himself while I stalked the snake from my console vantage perch with the paddle ready. I jabbed at him as he squirmed between my seat and the gas tank, holding him momentarily, but it only increased the moccasin's anger. He used all his strength to squirm out from my paddle hold, and headed for the stern. In a frantic effort to keep him from going in the bilge well, and then to safety under the deck where he would be impossible to rout out, I rammed the paddle against the snake's neck a few inches behind his head. The lick paid off. It paralyzed the moccasin for a moment, and I let him have a hard blow on the head. He folded, wriggled out his last breath, and finally lay lifeless on the deck.

Lindy and I looked at each other. It could have been a disaster. It would have been easy for the snake to have bitten my hand when I put bream after bream in the box. Then when the snake was mad and rampaging wild in the boat, we had no place to go except overboard. You are reluctant to abandon your boat a half mile from the shoreline, especially to an invading, poisonous snake.

It's a thousand wonders that snake's dangerous fangs didn't sink into my exposed legs. That mad moccasin tried everything to reach his tormentor. He really was obsessed with revenge.

We snapped a few pictures of the dead snake draped over the paddle. Finished with fishing for the day, we headed for home

Imprisoned By A Cottonmouth

with one thought for boat builders: Put a screen across livewell drains.

And don't wear shorts where cottonmouths abound. At least make the critter work to strike through your tough jeans or khakis. Those bare legs seem ever-so enticing to a mad snake looking for something to bury his fangs in.

If that cottonmouth could squeeze through and threaten us, there must be others with the same kind of determination. They are fond of tasty bream like those we had in the livewell and they will go to any lengths for food. We'd prefer they'd catch their own.

11

Winter In The Desert

by Larry Lazoen

There have been some terrible, cold winters in my native Illinois, but I can truthfully say I never have been as cold as I was on Lake Mead in the middle of one unforgettable July day.

When my partner and I began casting that morning, we were comfortable in shorts and T-shirts, the normal clothing for summertime fishermen on this massive lake 35 miles from Las Vegas. The temperature was a dry 111 degrees early in the day. Then it happened! In a matter of 15 minutes, the temperature dropped 40 degrees. We had no thermometer, so I don't know how cold it ultimately got. But when you are drenched to the skin, have no warm clothes to put on, and a 40-mile-an-hour wind rips across the water, the chill factor is way down. Any time the temperature falls so quickly, the drastic change is traumatic to the human body. A person can freeze at temperatures water won't.

In addition to the cold, hail as big as marbles rattled off the boat and our heads. Rain came down in sheets so heavy that I could hardly recognize my partner in the stern of the boat. The gale-force winds that swept over Lake Mead were frightening for any boater, novice or veteran. Known as "The Jewel of the Desert," this great bass-fishing haven with its high, rocky cliffs was suddenly a deadly foe for everyone on the water.

I realized that death by drowning was not my most immediate threat. Hypothermia was the real villain. My body temperature dropped below normal and my head began to pound. My vision was impaired and nausea swept over my whole system. I felt weak and faint. I knew that if I remained motionless, the cold would be fatal. I was shaking and trembling all over, as was my distraught partner. The wind was so strong that it seemed to drive the rain and hail right through my body.

Hypothermia had been the least of my worries in the middle of a desert in the summertime and I had come unprepared. I had no warm clothing in the boat, only a life jacket, as did my partner. We had put those on when the storm first hit, but they weren't enough to keep us from feeling like we had walked into a deep freezer. We were in trouble. There was no place to hide.

There had been no forecast of bad weather, and I wasn't sure what caused these devils of the desert. I read that they are unpredictable, occurring occasionally in hot arid areas when barometric pressure changes rapidly. Clouds form almost instantly, and good weather turns threatening without warning.

My muscles were out of control, further confirming that hypothermia was enveloping my body. I couldn't have cast a lure if I had wanted to. I couldn't even hold my fishing rod. I knew we were in real trouble when I was seized with a bone-chilling attack of shakes so violent that I had no balance. I couldn't stand on my feet. My partner was similarly weakened and fell to the deck.

With my body temperature out of kilter, I faced a horrible death in my beloved bass boat. I knew it would come very soon if I could not find a way to warm myself.

"Jump in! We can't survive in the boat," I yelled to my partner as he struggled to his feet. The water was very warm, near 90 degrees. If we could get in the water, and hang on to the side of the boat, we had a chance of beating the hypothermic death that stalked us.

I knew it was risky to leave the support of the boat, but if we hung on and didn't drown in the high wind, maybe we'd warm up. My partner agreed that we must do something and both of us plunged over the side. We were wearing good life jackets and we gripped the boat's gunnels. The warmth of the water permeated my body immediately and breathed new life into every muscle. Nothing ever felt as good as that warm water. It protected us from the chilling wind factor and restored our body temperatures to near normal.

I smiled for the first time since the unpredictable storm had rushed upon us. Staying submerged in the water was the answer. At least I hoped it was.

But our ordeal was far from over. The storm raged for three more hours while we hung precariously to the side of the rocking boat. The storm did not abate for a moment during those three hours. A constant gale drove rain and dangerous hail across the lake parallel to the water's surface. Holding on to the boat was not easy, but we were outdoorsmen with strength and stamina enough to last out the storm.

Then, almost as suddenly as it had begun, the winds ceased, the rain let up, and we climbed back into the disheveled boat. The hail hadn't harmed the fiberglass. The temperature shot up to 100 degrees again and the cold changed to hot sunshine. We picked up our tackle, adjusted the baits, and resumed the quest for keeper bass. It's amazing what a bass fisherman will do in a cast-for-cash tournament where there are big bucks for the winners.

Later in the afternoon when all the tournament contenders gathered at the weigh-in, the discussion was more about the storm than the usual fishing success and failure. Dozens of the pros had been caught without coats and warm clothing. They surmised, as we had, that survival meant jumping in the lake. They, too, took the plunge, hung on until the storm subsided, and survived hypothermia.

Miraculously, not a single fisherman had lingering ill effects from the experience. But it could have been wholesale disaster if we had not had the foresight and training to get relief in the warm water of Lake Mead. It was a last resort that saved us.

I no longer call Illinois home. I live at Port Charlotte in Florida. A three-time qualifier for the Bass Angler's Sportsman Society's BASS Master's Classic, I hope to keep on fishing the B.A.S.S. tournaments. But I don't want to go through another frightening experience like that one on Lake Mead. Nearly freezing to death in the summertime is simply not my cup of tea.

12

Don't Mess With Mama

by W. Horace Carter

everal years ago when I was fishing with some friends in Hanes Creek, near Leesburg, Florida, the peacefulness of the summer day was shattered when a man burst through the dense wilderness undergrowth. Panting for breath, he flopped down in a hammock that swung between two palm trees near the water. It was obvious that this squatter, who lived in the homemade shack where the hammock hung, was in trouble. He acted like he was being chased by the devil.

Disheveled and muddy from head to toe, the humbly dressed man was almost incoherent as he began to stutter and sputter. Was this the same creek-bank fisherman who had set up house-keeping here years ago and stayed?

"Man, am I lucky to be alive! I just had the closest call of my life. I thought for sure it was curtains this time," gasped the old reprobate. I had carelessly observed the man for years. His name was Jack Shumate, and he lived off the land and the lakes in a tiny lean-to house. It was built on a desolate knoll in the jungle-like wilderness off U.S. Highway 441, in Lake County, just south of Lake Griffin. He didn't know whose land he lived on, and didn't care as long as he was left alone.

Curious nearby anglers picked up their tackle and inched closer to hear more details about this narrow escape. What almost cost him his life? It ought to be an exciting revelation for this man was a character, always full of stories about his brushes with disaster during his decades of hermit-like existence.

"What happened? I saw you shove your boat off the hill, and head down the creek with your rod and reel about an hour ago," an interested kibitzer asked the frightened Shumate.

"It was too windy for me to fish the lake, and there was so many people around the locks at the highway that there wasn't really no room for me to fish from the bank. I needed some fish for my supper, so I decided to float down the creek, cast along the shoreline and see if I could latch on to a nice bucketmouth bass. There's usually plenty of them nesting in the shallows where there's lots of clean sand. I can usually catch a mess or two with a topwater in the dark shade of the willows. I fish them beds when the bass are making nests and gettin' ready to lay."

Shumate now had a captive audience, and he continued his story with dramatic flair. "I guess I'd moved about half a mile down the creek when I saw this big old mama alligator lyin' on her mud and brush mound where she had laid her eggs. She was nearly 12 feet long. Her eggs had hatched, and she was watching over a dozen or so 10-inch-long baby 'gators that were scooting all around her. Some of 'em were actually running in and out of her half-open mouth when they were scared. Mama 'gators sometimes swallow their young when they are trying to protect 'em. Maybe that's an accident.

"Now many people don't know that bass eat more alligators than alligators eat bass. But that's a fact. I've found many a small 'gator in the bellies of big bass I catch. They're a choice food for the largemouths in this here creek. With them baby 'gators movin' in and out of the water along the shoreline, I thought there might be a nice bass stalkin' a meal nearby. I've caught bass before around alligator nests, and this place sure looked like a good spot. I thought I'd give it a try.

"On my first cast a couple of feet from the bank, a bass rose to my plug, struck and missed. I think I jerked them hooks right out of her mouth. The splash annoyed the mama 'gator. She looked at the ripples, then at me, and went back to attending to her nursery problems. She didn't move from the mound, but I could see she was a little worked up. I didn't know just how worked up!"

Shumate acted out the next portion of his story with exaggerated gestures. "Encouraged with the strike, I flipped the big topwater in the same spot again. Nothing happened! I retrieved, and threw it a third time and plopped the plug down a foot nearer the 'gator nest than the first two. The old reptile raised her head a few inches, bellowed a slow warning snort, and then put her head back down. She rolled them big eyes toward me, her tormentor. I looked right back at her from my little homemade plywood boat. I should have learned something right then, but I did not.

"My next cast was a little wild. But I was distracted by the attention I was gettin' from the mama 'gator, and upset that I couldn't entice that bass to strike again. The big lure fell on the shoreline just inches from where two of the baby alligators were playing. They ran towards the plug. That enraged the 11-foot-long mama. She roared her disapproval, raised that mean ol' head with her dangerous teeth shinin', ran right over her offspring and plunged into the water, heading toward my little boat. I ain't never seen such a mad 'gator before. She was breathin' fire."

Shumate's voice grew to a high pitch. "I knew I was in big trouble, and I tried quick as I could to turn the boat away from the wake rushing toward me. It wasn't no use. No paddler can compete with a mad mama 'gator in the water, and I didn't have no motor on my boat."

Alligators are normally no threat to people, except when they

are raised in close proximity to man around parks where they are fed. But Shumate allowed as how he had pestered this big mama, causing her to surmise he was endangering her family. She had lost her patience and was after revenge. Shumate was her unfortunate target, and there was no way to get away from her.

"She surfaced a few feet from my boat and looked me straight in the eye. Was you ever eyeball to eyeball with a giant mama 'gator from a distance of five feet? Man, I tell you that is spooky. I've heard of people who looked at you so hard it seemed like they had daggers shootin' from their eyes. Well, that's what that old 'gator's eyes reminded me of. She seemed to be telling me, 'Brother, you ain't got no business throwin' that stuff around my babies. And you're gonna pay for it right now.'

"I never wanted to apologize for something so bad in my life. I was truly sorry. I didn't mean no harm. I was just tryin' to get a fish for supper."

Shumate looked truly penitent and was trembling slightly as he continued his tale. "Nothing registered with that mad old mama 'gator. She had used up all her patience with my first two casts. Now it was my behind she wanted; she'd get it now. Man, I was scared to death.

"She swung that long, deadly tail across the middle of my bateau. It splintered with that one whack as neat as if you'd used a big ax. I was surprised and scared to death. I could not believe that 'gator had ripped my boat in two. It sank in no time. I dog-paddled for a moment, frustrated and confused about what to do next. It didn't take me long to make up my mind. That 'gator stuck her snout out of the water only arm's length from my nose. She made the most gosh-awful bellow I ever heard come from any animal. It sounded like she was tellin' me, 'Your time is come. Say your last words before I tear you apart.' She paddled those short front legs a couple of times, and she was breathin' right in my face. I knew my number had come up.

"I forgot all about my rod, reel and tackle box and I headed for the west bank of the creek. It was about a hundred feet away. I could hear that old alligator right on my heels. I didn't dare look back to see if that big critter was gettin' ready to bite off a leg. I just knew any second might be my last. It sure made me a faster swimmer. I swum to that other shore so fast that I was wet on only one side when I got there."

Complete Angler's Library

A few of Shumate's listeners issued sounds of disbelief at his last comment, but he continued his story, unphased. "I struggled up the slick bank, panting and wheezing. I didn't look back when I hit the hill, but I knew she was still chasing me. I could hear her crashin' through the undergrowth and over the bushes. I was almost flying through the trees and bushes. She didn't even go around the bushes, she went over them, and for a few seconds I feared she'd catch me in spite of my record time over that rough obstacle course.

"I fell on my face twice and half expected her to be gnawin' on my legs before I got up. Then the noise stopped. I glanced behind me. She'd given up the chase. She was nowhere in sight. Apparently she'd decided I was no longer a threat to her little ones. But I was still shakin' with fright, and more wet with sweat than from my swimmin'. My heart felt like it was pounding hard enough to come right out of my chest.

"I was too scared to rest. That 'gator might come chargin' out of them bushes and still catch me. So, I just ran and ran until you saw me fight my way out of the brush over there a few minutes ago. I've never had such a close call. I'll think a long time before I pester another nesting mama alligator. They can have their privacy as far as I am concerned henceforth and forever more," expounded the fatigued old squatter.

Shumate had antagonized a mean old reptile enough to make her throw caution to the wind and take off after her persecutor. She almost caught him, and would have except for that fast swim and Olympic record dash through the swamp. Shumate's intrigued listeners began to wander back to their tackle.

"Would you like for us to carry you in my boat down the creek to see if you can find your tackle or salvage your boat?" one angler asked Shumate.

"No, thank you. I appreciate the offer. But the boat was cut completely in two and shattered beyond any hope of repair. My tackle sank in a deep hole just off from the 'gator nest. I sure don't want to go back there and irritate her again. Especially, I don't want to do it right now. Maybe in a day or two she'll cool off and I'll give it a look. Then again I might just let her have that equipment. It took me a lifetime to collect the stuff, but I don't believe it's worth bothering that old 'gator for.

"I've been livin' here about long enough. I might just pack up my bag, throw it in the ol' pickup, and look for another place to live. I get nervous when I live in the same spot a long time. And that mama 'gator just convinced me I had better move on," the squatter mumbled seriously.

Shaking their heads, his audience went back to fishing the creek bank for bass or anything else that would bite. But they couldn't forget the story of Shumate's narrow escape. It was a believe-it-or-not tale. Wet on only one side? That would be some real swimming, but who knows, any of us might be champions on land or water if we had a mad mama alligator snapping at our heels. At any rate, no one was going to try to disprove his story.

"Just to hear about it gives me the willies," said an old local as he cast a spoon near a half-submerged log in the current. Maybe there would be a lunker bass out there that wasn't near an alligator mound. He surely hoped so. He wasn't interested in an instant replay of Shumate's run-in with a guardian reptile.

A week after that encounter with Shumate on the shoreline in front of his shack, I was back fishing Hanes Creek again. His pickup was gone and the lean-to was empty. I asked a local fellow I had seen fishing there many times what happened to the squatter.

"The day after he told us about swimming the creek and not getting wet on but one side, he packed up everything and took off. We have no idea where he was headed. He just wanted to get away from that mama alligator. He was afraid she might come up the creek and hunt him up. At least that's what he told some fellows who stayed around to hear more about his narrow escape," the old codger said with a sly grin on his face. "Wet on only one side," he mumbled, shaking his head. "I'd like to have seen that chase."

13

Horror In Brazil

by J. P. Garner

There is a species of pink, blind dolphins, also known as bouto, which has rarely been observed by modern man. A few years ago, I enthusiastically accepted a challenge to head a year-long expedition into the Brazilian interior, the Mato Grosso, to capture some of the pretty creatures for a zoological attraction in the nation's capital city, Brasilia.

As a naturalist, I felt it would be rewarding to help create a fantastic spectacle for tourists from around the world to observe. Nowhere else on the planet would there be a zoological observatory featuring these unique creatures. The wonderfully clear water in the natural zoological volcanic aquarium would showcase my effort and skills for years. It would give me a chance to leave my mark on the world. At 43 years of age, this opportunity seemed to be the fulfillment of a life-long dream.

A group of Brazilian businessmen hired me to supervise construction of a 4,000-acre, fenceless wildlife compound in the surrounding jungle near Brasilia, and to establish native fish and animals in a natural park. They gave me specific instructions to go into the Mato Grosso wilderness, and capture about 300 of the stranger-than-fiction blind dolphins that were to be found only in the most remote and desolate spots on the Araguaia River.

The promoters of the zoological aquarium and wildlife compound promised to underwrite all of my expenses and that of a four-man crew of laborers. Once I had reached my destination, they would fly in with medicines and food twice a month, and would also pay me a pretty penny for successfully tackling and completing the project.

The Mato Grosso wilderness is hundreds of thousands of square miles of unexplored, almost impenetrable jungle occupied by a few disease-afflicted natives. In fact, the Mato Grosso is so dense that the geographical center of Brazil was not reached until 1958, and few early explorers in that region ever returned to civilization. But it was the only place where these freshwater dolphins existed in nature.

The United States Embassy in Brasilia advised me not to make the trip. They insisted it was dangerous. But I was determined, stubborn and anxious to be a pioneering hero in the 20th century. So my crew and I loaded the 24-foot pontoon boat with good fishing tackle, nets and the supplies required for our unique expedition into the wilderness.

We began the Mato Grosso adventure by heading into the north-flowing Araguaia River 600 miles from the mouth of the Amazon. It was a wild-water fantasy course, and a sportsman's paradise. We caught fish that didn't have names but were gourmet eating. They would bite anything dead or alive that we put on a hook and dropped into the water. Despite the fact that my Portuguese crewmen could not speak a word of English, the first few weeks of the adventure were reasonably enjoyable. We happily sampled the food, and drank in the novelty of exploring a beautiful, unspoiled wilderness. Had we envisioned the threats we would encounter, we might not have enjoyed ourselves so freely.

Once we reached the jungle area where the pink, blind dolphins were known to live, I had to make my own traps from vines, limbs and trees. I designed them after those of my teacher, the late Dr. John N. Hamlet. He had built cages in the Philippines to capture the 5,000 cynomulgus monkeys used in experiments that eventually perfected the polio vaccine. The traps would capture the dolphins safely without injuring them.

We set up near a native Indian village known as Bandeirant where about 80 semi-civilized, hunter-fishermen lived. There was a small clearing where little puddle-jumping airplanes could land. That was my main reason for holding the dolphins at this point of the river. We could get food and medicines from our suppliers before starting the long, hard trip back to Brasilia with the precious live cargo.

We immediately began the challenging task of trapping the blind, pretty creatures. Their eyes were small and shrunken, as eyesight was not much use in this murky, turgid water. But they had a high sonar dome and hearing like radar, making it nearly impossible to sneak up on them. Their long beaks were lined top and bottom with sharp teeth that threatened our hands and feet. The dolphins grew to a length of 10 feet and weighed up to 600 pounds. The young ones were grayish in color and as they matured they became pink.

We worked around the clock for several weeks and managed to trap 300 fine specimens. My crew and I corralled them in a rubber-coated, steel fence attached to strong PVC pipe around the pontoon boat. At that point it appeared that we could claim success. But it was not to come so easily.

The promised shipments of food and supplies never materialized. We had to catch food or die. We fought armadas of mosquitoes and other insects day and night. The medications were exhausted too. My bosses had either forgotten us, or couldn't find us in the jungle labyrinth. We would be hard to spot even with the village nearby.

Sick and depressed, I didn't think things could get much worse. Then one morning I got up to find my crew gone. I presume they stole a crude boat from some of the jungle natives, and headed upriver toward Brasilia. Or they may have tried to walk out of the jungle over a pig-path road that wound through desert, dangerous watery swamps and mountains for 1,000 miles. I don't know what their fate was; I never saw them again. I cursed them in absentia for leaving, but couldn't blame them.

With my crew gone, I faced almost insurmountable problems. Each of my 300 pink dolphins ate from 12 to 30 pounds of fish per day. That takes a lot of fishing, even where millions of forage species thrive. With the help of Poao Pinto, the mayor of the village, and his son, I struggled to keep the dolphins healthy. Working from daylight to dark, we dumped thousands of fish into the cage every day.

I discovered that the dolphins preferred the meat-eating, vicious piranha for food. Piranha will attack men and cut them to shreds. We trapped the piranha in shallow, fast-running water. If they catch you in deep water they'll strip the meat from your bones. Despite the danger of catching the piranha, I went after them with traps and nets and fed thousands to the dolphins. I ate the piranha too and found it to be a flavorful fish. They would bite any kind of meat I put on a hook, but were slow to hit artificial lures.

There were other dangers I faced in trapping fish for the dolphins. There were millions of small critters that looked like tiny catfish. In the rainy season, which lasted most of the time I was in that jungle, these killers entered any human opening they could find. After entering the body, they ate their hapless victims from the inside out, resulting in a painful death. Quick surgery to remove the deadly creatures provided the only hope of survival.

There was also a species of huge catfish that thrived in the muddy, deep water. They reached weights of up to 700 pounds. They tore many of my nets to shreds when they became trapped with the dolphins. Several times they also destroyed the 55-gallon steel drums that we used for floats. They crushed them so that they leaked and sank. These big cats were good to eat, but they could eat their captors too. I know that I have never fought a marlin, sailfish, shark, cobia, salmon or any other giant fish in fresh or saltwater that had the power of that monster-size catfish. I hooked many of them just for sport. While I enjoyed eating some fine fillets from the catfish we managed to trap, I never got one to the gunnels on a line. They simply had too much power for my 120-pound test mono. I often fought one for hours, only to see it break everything and take off down the river when it got tired of being on the hook.

The river provided another danger when it was flooding—unbelievable erosion. Once I was out on the river trying to catch food for the dolphins with a young native I called Edgar. Heavy rains had sent flood waters dashing down through the jungle. In absolute awe, we watched a mile-long, 40-foot high sandbar crumble and melt into the river.

Giant shoreline trees were constantly undermined by the erosion as well, causing them to plummet into the swift current. These 100-foot tall trees swept down the river, trapping and drowning many of the natives. Indeed, death was so commonplace in the village that when a fisherman or hunter didn't show up at the end of the day, he was presumed dead. No one bothered to look for him. The river swallowed people up without a trace.

The natives believed that a baby thrown into the river would return as a giant snake and claim revenge (they often threw newborns into the river when the father was in question). They ground up the teeth of the piranha for pregnant women to eat as a remedy for childbirth pain. Maybe there were pain-killing properties in the piranha teeth or maybe not; at any rate, the mothers claimed it worked.

Temperatures during the daylight hours were miserable, but nights would have been almost pleasant except for the hordes of insects. I had brought 15 good mosquito nets with me on the trip and suspended them from the ceiling of my boat with ropes. I expected to be protected from the mosquitoes and other stinging insects. But the nets and even the ropes that held them over me were quickly eaten up by hungry beetles.

I brought cases of insect repellent along. Perspiration in the humid climate washed it away quickly; the very best lasted no longer than 15 minutes. A paste made by the natives from roots was better than the chemical repellents, but it too was effective for only a short time. It looked like glue and the insects stuck in the gooey mess by the thousands. With one swipe of my hand, I could wipe a cup full of mosquitoes off my body any night. Only by running the gasoline-powered pump on the boat, turning on the shower, and then lying on the floor with my nose and mouth outside, could I get any relief from the insects. Unfortunately, the shower also pumped up waterborne pests—so I soon gave up on that idea.

The carnivorous insects were all sizes and they could find their way through any obstacle. I could not keep them out of the boat. I rigged a crude insect trap that I hoped would reduce their numbers and provide me with a little relief. It was a lighted, kerosene lantern mounted on top of a fuel barrel that was half full of oily water. It worked well and in a single night I could collect 10 pounds of insects in the barrel trap. But the supply was endless and they continued to eat me alive.

Nearly as bad as the mosquitoes was another hated insect— the white wasp. It was similar to a scorpion and was a rapacious assailant. Sometimes five or six would pounce on me at the same time. I endured many terribly painful bites from them.

The weeks of working long hours trying to feed myself and the dolphins while fighting insects, the weather and illness had dragged me down. Disappointed and angry that my employers had

Complete Angler's Library

apparently abandoned me, I inventoried my predicament.

I had arrived at the Mato Grosso a robust 205-pound man. I was now a skinny 130 pounds and nearly delirious from constant high fever. I realized that I was not only going to lose my precious dolphins to starvation, but lose my own life. With my blood being sucked out by more than a thousand species of painful bugs, wracked with malaria, dysentery and other tropical diseases, I knew I could survive only a few more days. I would never see my wife and daughter at Homosassa Springs, Florida, again.

With tears flooding my cheeks, I talked with God like I never had before. I needed help, divine help, and I needed it now. You may scoff and doubt. I wouldn't blame you. You will probably think, "Oh, he was out of his head with the fever and he let his imagination run away with him." But the experience was as real to me then as it is now. God heard those prayers, and He saw my plight. He told me to hang on a few more days. I would escape this death that had me in its clutches.

Time raced by. In my delirium, time came and went in waves. I couldn't tell if two hours or two weeks passed. But one morning I heard the sweet drone of a single-engine plane. I struggled outside and waved. The pilot saw me. Minutes later he put the plane down on the narrow, weed and bush-clad strip. My native friends put me aboard after promising to do everything they could to keep my blind dolphins healthy. They had been such great helpers!

My employers were apologetic. They had tried repeatedly to find me, they said. Luckily, one pilot had expanded the search and almost by accident spotted my waving arms and the boat.

After a few days of fever treatment in Brasilia, I was carried aboard a commercial plane and flown back to Florida into the waiting arms of my wife Sandra and daughter Dawn. It was a most rewarding reunion. Many times in the jungle I had dreamed of this moment, and many times believed it was lost forever.

Eventually, an expedition was sent back into the Mato Grosso after my dolphins. The natives had kept them alive and healthy. The dolphins were transported to the zoological garden in Brasilia. Thousands of people drive in from the surrounding area to view them every day.

14

My War With
The Poachers

by Walter Burrell

oachers saw the foot-long piece of railroad iron ricochet off the surface of Rock Lake, and the six men illegally setting gillnets by the light of the moon heard the lethal missile ripping through the tops of trees on the distant shoreline. They dropped everything, high-tailed it out of there, and never again bothered my private fishing hole.

That was a long time ago, but I still remember that night like it was yesterday. The experience was delightful for me then and now. Even though I am approaching 90, I wear a satisfied smile when I think back on that memorable evening.

I left my native Montana in a canoe in 1928, and paddled it all the way to Tampa, Florida. I followed some of the same route of the early American explorers, Lewis and Clark, and was intrigued with many of the desolate waterways I saw on that rigorous, six-month boating adventure.

Many of the places at which I stopped on my trip appeared to have never before been trod by white men. American Indians inhabited the swamps and parts of the hill country, but few if any whites ever saw the beautiful sights that I marveled at on my solitary journey.

The countryside—the hills, marshes and swamps and the vast expanse of water of the Gulf of Mexico—was all new to a young man from the mountains and plains of Montana. And, paddling a canoe let me see it all, close up. I could stop and wet a line any time I wanted to, and some of the fish I pulled in were never heard of in my home state. But I kept going, wanting to see what was around the next bend until I reached Florida!

Always a fisherman and outdoorsman, I searched the Tampa Bay area for a homesite that would fulfill my needs. My choice was a few acres on the banks of Rock Lake near the community of Odessa. Experienced in farming, I knew I could grow crops on the virgin land, and there were plenty of bass, bluegills and crappies in the lake that had never seen an angler's bait. It was a desolate area, so it was seldom fished. I cleared about 30 acres of land, and began farming and fishing to eke out a humble living for myself and later for the family I raised on the Rock Lake shoreline.

Florida's population began to explode in the late 1930s. More and more vehicles chugged down the little pigpath dirt road that passed by my farm. I was used to plowing my fields stark naked, since it kept me cooler in the summer. Much to my dismay, as the traffic increased and civilization crept in, I had to wear overalls.

Observing the pretty lake behind my house, fishermen rightly conjectured that it must be full of fish. Soon I began hearing commotions on the lake late at night, so I paddled my boat out to investigate one evening, and discovered poachers setting gillnets and dragging in bushels of gamefish in long seines. I was mad as heck to see the fish caught in such an unsportsmanlike manner.

There were no wildlife laws back then, and even if there were, no one would have enforced them. I had to stop this wholesale destruction or my lake wouldn't provide meals for my family. So, I kindly told the midnight anglers they would have to stop setting nets and catching my fish.

The poachers just laughed at me. They said the fish belonged to them just as much as they did to me, and they would keep right on "fishing." They said I couldn't do a damn thing about it. Thoroughly angered at their snotty arrogance, I advised them not to come back. I would protect Rock Lake myself because there were no game wardens to do it. They continued to scoff and ignore my warnings. Those guys were downright abusive and insulting, definitely not good people.

I was lucky. They could have turned my boat over and drowned me that night. They didn't do that, but they sure gave me a lot of lip. I decided right then and there that I wouldn't let them ruin my lake. Even if what I had in mind might be considered rather drastic. I had to fight fire with fire.

The next day I started making what I called a "fieldpiece." Today it might be more accurately described as a crude, homemade cannon. I bolted a strong, five-foot steel barrel on two metal wheels to make it portable. Then I rigged up a firing mechanism on the gun. It was finished. I sat back to admire my handiwork, then moved the unique weapon into my lakeside barn. I could get it in place quickly if the need arose though it did look awkward in the barn loft.

I waited for the return of the arrogant poachers. The way they scoffed at my warning, I was sure they would be back sooner or later. They thought I had been intimidated.

Several weeks passed, and I began to think maybe I had successfully scared the illegal fishermen off. Then on the night of a harvest moon, I again heard talking and laughing out on the lake. I walked to the shoreline, and I could clearly see several men setting gillnets near the center of the lake. I surmised it must be the same six that I had warned not to return. The day of reckoning had arrived. I relished that moment and wore a wide smile as I made my move to discourage them.

This time I didn't go out to ask them to leave. I went to the barn, and rolled my heavy cannon to the cypress-clad lake bank. I positioned it to my satisfaction. It would do the job at the elevation I had it set. At last my math and physics at the University of Montana were going to pay off.

I poured about a half-gallon of black powder down the barrel and after stuffing in some packing, I inserted a foot-long piece of railroad iron that I had secured for a missile. I pointed it in the general direction of the poachers, and elevated the barrel enough to make sure it would make the distance. Then I struck a match to the fuse. The cannon roared.

I have never heard such a loud blast as that fieldpiece made. It was like a close thunderclap. Black smoke boiled up all around me and the gun. The fieldpiece recoiled at least five feet, and almost broke my legs in the process. It would certainly have crippled me had it hit me.

That railroad missile hit right in the midst of the poachers, but it had so much power at that slight angle that it bounced off the water and headed for the distant shoreline. I could hear, and I am sure the poachers could hear, the projectile cutting off the tops of the sweetgum and cypress trees a half-mile away. I don't know where it finally stopped, but it was sure one fine makeshift projectile for scaring poachers.

That one shot did the trick. The poachers scrambled for the west bank away from my side of the lake as fast as they could paddle. They didn't even bother to retrieve the nets they had strung out all over the lake. If ever a man had a gleam in his eye, I had it that night. Success was written all over my wrinkled face.

It is easy to understand why the poachers chose never to return to Rock Lake. It's one thing to get shot, but it's an entirely different thing when you are nearly hit by a missile in the middle of the night. I think my remedy for discouraging poachers was a good idea. I stored my gun in the attic of the barn where it has been idle for about half a century. It has almost rusted away from lack of activity in fending off poachers.

I kind of expected a sheriff to come by and ask about the incident, but no officer ever appeared. I suspect anyone going to the sheriff and reporting a cannonball being fired at them from the shoreline would be suspected of boozing it up too much. Poachers were often drunk when they made their hauls.

A lot has changed since then. There are fishermen on Rock

Lake virtually every day now, and I accept that. The fishing today is mostly hook and line and legal, and the newcomers have as much right to harvest the resource as I do. People now live on "my" lake. Over the years, more than a dozen nice lake homes have joined my original farmstead on Rock Lake. That little pig-path dirt road is now paved, and civilization has surrounded my beautiful lake. And, there are laws that protect the game fish, making those early activities illegal and very expensive for those who are caught.

But I have no apologies for firing my cannon at a bunch of poachers who were decimating the lake a generation ago.

=15=

Two Rogues In A Row

by Capt. Pete Sommerville

Sunrise was still half an hour away when I began the most unforgettable fishing trip of my life. We shoved off from the Little Salmon River in New York at 5:30 a.m. for a day of chinook salmon fishing in Lake Ontario's Mexico Bay. I had a first mate and four enthusiastic passengers. Our honey hole was about 12 miles from the marina and we had been having considerable success with salmon in the 25-30 pound range.

At daybreak I had listened to the weather reports. The forecasts were for continued good weather. Always cautious, I followed up the public weather news by phoning for additional information. Those reports were good too. With a normal one- to two-foot chop, all was well.

We looked forward to a peaceful day on one of the beautiful Great Lakes where the transplanted salmon return after three years. The first salmon from the released, transplanted stock came back in 1976. The catch success has been excellent ever since. In fact, 105 charter boat captains have moved from Lake Michigan to the New York base since then to reap the rewards of the fishing bonanza.

On the way to our fishing spot, I was surprised to see the waves were picking up, some as high as four feet. I radioed for the most recent weather reports. The news was unchanged. The wind would lie down. The seas would go flat. I hoped the forecasts were reliable.

Between 8 and 9 a.m., we trolled through a school of chinooks, quickly landing four. We lost several other fish that spit their hooks. It was a fast and furious hour. My anglers were happy and excited by the fishing action. They were in for more!

Soon after, two outside lines popped from the outriggers. I yelled for the passengers to grab the rods, knowing the moment I saw those strikes that these kings were larger than the four we had boated. It would take time, patience and a little expertise to land them, especially because the waves continued to build, and my angling clients were having difficulty maintaining their balance on the rocking deck of the boat.

The four-foot waves were too much for all the smaller boats in the area and they disappeared, despite the tremendous fishing. I was apprehensive and again radioed for weather forecasts. Nothing had changed. Abating wind and calm seas were assured, but the clouds and rising wind we were experiencing seemed foreboding and contradictory.

My clients continued to fight the two big salmon on the lines. I was reluctant to cut them off after they had worked so hard, but I knew we had to get out of there. The waves were now six feet high, and the wind had picked up drastically. My boat must have looked like a bobber as the swells rose.

Nervously, I kept maneuvering the Trojan for another 10 minutes. By then, the anglers had landed one fine 30-pound king salmon and lost the other. I yelled for the mate to secure the tackle, and for all of them to get below. I revved up the engine from my 14-foot high seat on the flying bridge, and headed for port. I sensed it might not be a cakewalk. Winds had reached 45 miles an hour or more. Waves were running eight feet high.

To make it worse, I had to put the swells on the stern of the boat when we headed for port. A following sea makes handling the boat more difficult, but with 12 years of experience, I knew I could guide us back to shore on a big craft like my Trojan. I wished I had started in earlier, but how do you tell clients to quit fighting a big fish and reel in the line?

The huge waves came in from the stern, slid under the boat and we fell into the trough, often with a loud, splashing bang. It was nerve-racking for my passengers who were not used to such wild water and wind, but I was slowly steering us to the marina. I had some trouble handling the boat when a few 12-foot waves hit us, but my experience and the sturdiness of the boat kept us mov-

Complete Angler's Library

ing along, albeit rather slowly.

Then I saw the danger approaching. A rogue wave was a few yards away. I knew it was at least 14 feet high because it was eye level with my seat on the flying bridge. These bigger, rougher waves often pose a problem for small boats, but normally present no danger for a 30-footer like my Trojan. What made this dangerous was a rare phenomenon. Two rogue waves together, a once-in-a-lifetime occurrence, were sweeping down on our stern. I had never seen two together before. I watched awestruck, nearly paralyzed, as they approached with relentless power.

The first one hit like an avalanche. Its great force pushed the boat around like a dry wood chip. The Trojan was sideways, cockeyed in the watery trough. The second rogue was sweeping in before there was time to right the boat and get it perpendicular to the on-rushing wall of water. From below I could hear my frightened passengers, two of whom were in their 60s, screaming as they held on to everything they could grasp to keep from being bounced off the bulkheads.

I knew they were in danger of sustaining injuries from being tossed about. I wished I could help them, but at that moment, my attention was on righting the boat—fearing flooding and drowning as the second giant wave hit the boat broadside. I had not been able to point the bow into the first wave. We were in a predicament!

In a split second, the boat was listing almost 90 degrees. The bottom of the boat was near the top of the swell, and I was only inches from the water as the flying bridge went over. I scribed an arc of 22 feet on my sweep down near the surface and back upright again. Water rushed in all over the deck, and if we hadn't swung back upright almost instantly, it would have been curtains for all of us. If the Trojan had not been equipped with the flying bridge and its added top weight, we would have bellied-up right there. But the boat righted itself, and I knew then that the flying bridge was a good trade-off for the decreased stability the high structure creates in less threatening seas.

With the two rogue waves leaving us, I quickly got the boat perpendicular to the swells. Now my worries for the safety of the passengers and crew returned. They could have easily been swept overboard when the deck flooded. Maybe I was a lone survivor of the fateful trip.

Two Rogues In A Row

Then I heard frantic voices. Jerry Passer and his wife Carol were asking each other how they had fared. Jerry had a badly bruised arm from being tossed around. Carol had been sitting in a deck chair with a stranglehold on a cabin rail when the second wave hit us. The chair flew out from under her and crashed against the far wall, but she tenaciously hung on to the boat's railing. When it was over, she was dangling precariously to the strong railing, frightened but unhurt. She later said she was "prepared to say goodbye to the world."

Dr. John Foster and his wife Gwen, a pair of middle-aged anglers, reacted a little faster. Each had grabbed hold of a rail in time to keep from being bounced and bruised. Gwen lost her hold with one hand, but tightened her grip and hung on with the other. Neither suffered anything but fright from the near-capsizing. I'm sure they were full of thanksgiving.

"I think we were all lucky," Dr. Foster acknowledged.

But the danger did not all pass with the rogues. The boat was extremely sluggish with the hull half-filled with water. We suddenly were drafting at least 10 more inches. The added weight and reduced freeboard would be a problem if another big wave swept over the stern. I held my breath, expecting the worst.

Fifteen critical minutes later, after dozens of 10- to 12-foot swells had pounded the stern and slid under the heavy hull, I knew we were going to make it. We would not be claimed by Lake Ontario's Grim Reaper—the same Force that takes nearly 10 lives every year.

A lucky repair job I had done some months before probably saved the Trojan and its human cargo. Two, 1,200-gallon-per-hour, high-capacity pumps that the boat was originally equipped with might not have unloaded water fast enough to keep us afloat in that storm. One of the pumps had broken down, and I removed and replaced it. Later, I repaired the original malfunctioning pump and installed it in the boat too. The three hard-working pumps got us back on an even keel rather quickly in the storm, and we navigated back to a berth at the marina without any further complications.

I have always had great respect for the weather. I take special precautions when my instincts and observations seem to warn me that all is not well with the elements. The information I got was faulty, and that is all the more reason charter boat skippers and

other fishermen should constantly be aware that no weather forecasts are ever guaranteed. There are always exceptions that may kill you. Two rogue waves side by side are as rare as sighting an albino whale. Such a killer wave in a storm usually sweeps down no more than once in a hundred. We had two hit us broadside within a few seconds. It is hard to prepare for that rare exception.

Even though we normally fish only 11 miles from the port, the way storms can brew up in a matter of minutes here makes it risky for the 17- to 18-foot open boats that often converge nearby. It's not unusual to see an armada of these small boats way out in Lake Ontario. I can say for sure, had we been out there on that frightening August morning in a small boat, I would not be here to write about it.

Our survival pivoted upon the trusty 30-foot Trojan swinging upright quickly, even while burdened with tons of extra water weight—and the fortunate, almost accidental, installation of the third and now very important bilge pump.

There are other dangers in a big body of water like Lake Ontario, especially in the northern climates. Hypothermia has claimed the lives of many fishermen when sudden weather changes caught them without enough protective clothing to maintain their normal body temperature.

But for me, the two unique rogue waves pouring down upon us almost simultaneously provided the most life-threatening adventure I have ever endured. I don't expect or hope to have any repeat performance of that dreadful day.

16

Walking Into My Own Wake

by Sam Petit

G ale-force winter winds ripped across Lake Waccamaw in southeastern North Carolina, and I realized my tiny boat was no match for this dangerous storm. Head-high waves were dashing gallon after disastrous gallon into my homemade fishing machine, which was already half filled with water. Once full, I knew the outboard and my weight would be too much for the plywood craft to stay afloat. Then it would be sink or swim. With the shoreline at least two miles away, I wouldn't make it.

I had looked forward to this December day. The morning rain gave me reason to cancel my work plans for completing the masonry wall on a big warehouse I was building, and that meant I could go fishing in the afternoon. As I often told friends, "I never get to fish on a pretty day. I work then. I get to fish all the bad days." Rain, heat, cold and wind never stopped me fishing.

I drove my pickup to gin-clear Lake Waccamaw off Highway 74, east of Whiteville, North Carolina, in Columbus County. Waccamaw is a natural lake created thousands of years ago when a giant meteor knocked a big hole in the Green Swamp, then burned itself out. Waccamaw Indians lived on this lake and enjoyed its resources for countless centuries. I lifted my handmade ultralight, nine-foot plywood boat from my truck, and slid it easily into the beautiful lake. I glanced around at the sky and took note of some ominous cloud formations in the west.

I had fished bad weather all of my adult life. I was not only an experienced fisherman in all these freshwaters, I was a pretty good seaman. I could handle this little boat with a short, light paddle in almost any kind of wind and waves. Besides, with a definite front approaching, this might be the very best time of the year for me to fill my creel with fine white perch. Fish seem to instinctively understand fronts and often go into a feeding frenzy shortly before bad weather hits. I was eager to take advantage of the pattern.

With my tackle box and rods and reels in the boat, I pushed off from the white, sandy shoreline where giant cypress trees grew well out into the lake, and climbed into my boat. Despite my 200 pounds, I was agile, and made it over the gunnels like a monkey without dipping a single drop of water over the skimpy freeboard.

Observers of my little fishing boat often called it a "floating coffin," and cautioned me that they wouldn't be caught dead in such a tiny contraption on a lake like Waccamaw that had a reputation for quickly getting very rough. Its shallowness, averaging only six feet, made it wild when strong winds rushed in from the north and west. But I laughed at the fearmongers. I had fished this lake for three decades and had faced a lot of bad weather. My boat and I were inseparable. We could handle the inclimate conditions, and still catch a mess of fish for the family for supper.

I yanked on the crank rope, and the 5-horsepower outboard came alive. I opened it up, and headed downwind toward the south end of the lake where the grass beds were plentiful. I decided to try the perch first around that aquatic cover. I had discovered that these perch loved pandemonium. The more splashing and commotion you made on the surface, the more fish you could catch. They would always come to a noise and then strike anything you flaunted in their faces. I knew this technique worked best on a calm day, but perhaps before the waves got higher they would still succumb to my spinners and wet flies.

Cutting the engine 50 yards from a house-size grass bed, I began beating my paddle in the water. The waves were really kicking up. I glanced back from where I launched the boat. Two boats were being loaded. The other fishing boats had already left the lake. I was alone.

Bingo! A big white perch hit my Mepps spinner. I didn't have to set the hook. The near 2-pounder swallowed everything. That's a real monster size for white perch in Lake Waccamaw. They normally run from about 12 ounces to a pound. I figured the big ones must be feeding in anticipation of the front.

Instant replay continued for half an hour. I boated a fine stringer of perch, the largest on average I had ever caught. I wished I had some friends out here now. Later they wouldn't believe my success story. I soon reiterated that wish—but for other reasons.

A gust of wind hit the boat broadside, spinning it around like a corn cob in a blizzard. For the first time, the approaching storm got my attention. This was no illusion. This was the real thing. It was unusual to have a hurricane in December, but that gust sure seemed like it meant business. I lay my rod down gently in the bottom of the boat and appraised my situation.

It would probably blow over in an hour or so, I thought. I decided to run down to the southern shoreline and wait it out. Many times in the summer when squalls hit while I was on the lake, I had tied up to the shoreline trees, covered up with a poncho, and waited out the blow.

I pulled on the outboard crank rope at the very instant a super wave flopped over the stern, engulfing not only the engine but the whole boat. It was suddenly half full of water. I quickly jerked the rope again and again. It was no use. The water had wet the plugs. It would take a lot of drying out before I could crank the motor again.

Strong as an ox from having lifted hundreds of cement blocks all my life on masonry jobs, I picked up the paddle and headed toward the nearest trees.

The storm was coming in whirlwind fashion. Wind gusts of 60 miles per hour swept down every few minutes from the west, then shifted to the east or south. Every time I got within a half mile or so of a shoreline, the wind changed and carried me back into the middle of the lake. The winds were getting stronger by the minute and I began to realize that I was in serious trouble. My feet were in ankle-deep water. Every wave was splashing more water into the boat. Darkness was approaching as well, aggravating my already grave situation.

I got scared as the reality of my predicament struck me. There was not another boat on the lake. I couldn't get to the shoreline. The boat was almost full of water, and I knew that it would not support me and the other weight once it was full. Maybe this would be my coffin after all, I thought.

I made a decision then that might not have occurred to most boaters. Since most sophisticated factory crafts are unsinkable even when flooded, the advice for endangered passengers is usually to hang on to the side of the boat. Unfortunately, my boat had no styrofoam or space compartments that would keep it afloat. It would sink quickly once it had water over the gunnels.

While I hated to lose my tackle box, rods, reels and the fine mess of fish I had boated, I realized that I was going to drown in that hurricane if I didn't do something drastic, fast. I slipped off my shoes, jumped overboard, and turned the boat upside down, pouring everything into the lake.

I made the boat flip as quickly as I could so that I trapped plenty of air under it. With that buoyancy, it was like a cork in the waves. I knew if I could keep that air trapped, at least the boat wouldn't sink. I climbed on the boat, and grabbed the gunnels in each hand, lying flat on my belly.

Many times in the next few hours I almost lost that bubble. I heard the gurgling noise of the escaping air when giant waves tossed the boat and me around like a heron feather. It was a sound that I didn't want to hear. Each time I heard it my apprehension grew because I knew that the only chance I had was tied to my boat staying on top of the water. All I could do was pray that enough air would stay trapped to keep me and my little boat afloat.

If my arms hadn't been so muscled from handling heavy blocks and bricks, I could never have hung on. Hanging on to that upside-down boat in six- and seven-foot waves was worse than riding a bucking bronco. I got seasick and so tired that my arms felt like they would break. I prayed, cried and talked to myself. That helped pass the time as the storm did not abate, and my chances seemed nil. I shivered and shook in the cold and wind, and clung to that upside-down boat.

It was midnight when my spirits reached their lowest level. I kept washing around in circles, the wind constantly shifting, and not getting any closer to the shoreline. The darkness was frightening. I had had no idea where I was in the lake for hours. What hope did I have?

Unknown to me, when I had failed to show up at home at dinner-time, my son and neighbors, suspecting that the bad storm might have caught me on the lake, drove to Waccamaw hoping to find me. They launched their big boats at the dock to go searching, but the giant waves quickly filled those crafts with water. They couldn't go anywhere.

About 9 o'clock, they called the rescue squad, reporting their worst fear, that I must have drowned. Experienced rescue boaters arrived. They looked at the churning waves.

"There is no way we can go out on that lake now. Even our largest boats wouldn't be able to make it. I hate to say it, but there is no way anyone could survive out there on a nine-foot bateau. That raging lake is no place for a one-man boat. That's a wild lake. We better notify Sam's family that he is lost. We'll start looking for the body in the morning," the squad leader said. Then he sent a courier to pass along the sad news to my wife and family.

"Some of us will stay here so we can start searching as soon as it is safe and daylight," a rescuer said, in an effort to provide some hope for my family.

Just before midnight, the sad news was told to my wife, who was already apprehensive. Other relatives were called, and they mourned through the night and past dawn.

Meantime, I continued to shiver and shake. The cold, and the knowledge that any minute might be my last, were frightening. I had a little relief when I saw the first faint rays of a cold morning sun peaking through the overcast sky.

Almost as suddenly as it had swooped down upon me, the gusts subsided. Calmness came with the dawn and the sun. And, an even more beautiful sight! Land! The most desolate shoreline on the lake was only a few hundred yards away. I smiled and began dog-paddling feverishly with renewed energy toward safety. My little boat had remained afloat, but now it just seemed to inch along as my hands pushed at the water. But, move it did. Nothing could stop me now.

It was a wonderful feeling when that boat first scraped the bottom. I could hardly stand erect, but I staggered to the hill, and dragged my little floating coffin onto the sand. I prayed with real thanksgiving in every word. It was a blessing to be alive, notwithstanding the long trek I was going to have to make through the snakes and alligators in Tar Heel State swamp.

Luckily, I didn't have to make that walk. Rescue boats raced around the lake as soon as it was safe. They were surprised to see a tall, gangling fisherman waving wildly from the southern shoreline. Moments later they picked me up, secured my overturned boat so it could be retrieved later, wrapped me in a couple of blankets, and rushed back to the dock. I insisted that I didn't need any medical attention. Just notify my family that I am okay, I insisted, and take me home. I would do my recuperating there. I just wanted to be home with my family, and I couldn't wait to get there.

Efforts to notify my family of the rescue were futile. The telephone lines were busy as friends and relatives were telling others of the disastrous misfortune of the Petits. I learned later that the phone had seldom rested during the night as my family and friends gave each other support.

The ride home seemed to take forever, but in reality it was

only a few minutes. What was that compared to the long hours of torture I'd just been through. Now, at 10 a.m., nearly 24 hours later, I walked through the front door of my home to my own wake. Despair turned to explosive joy. Never had there been so much hugging and kissing as took place on that happy morning. It was like a resurrection.

Later the same day friends pulled my boat back home. I still cherish it as the finest fishing machine you can find on Lake Waccamaw. Still, maybe I should have been a little more cautious when I saw that front moving in. A little boat can only take so much. When I only have bad days in which to fish, I've had a ten-

dency to minimize the danger presented by those fast-moving dark clouds that often are accompanied by gale-force winds. I'll think twice now when a storm's brewing.

It was so good to be a survivor, to be alive. Perhaps I can get back after those white perch before long. I sure hope so. At least this horrible experience didn't take away my life-long desire to fish at every opportunity.

As soon as some more bad weather arrives, I'll be back on Lake Waccamaw in my same little boat. But, it will be with greater respect for what nature can do.

17

The Nine Lives Of Hoyt Ergle

by W. Horace Carter

T ragedy struck Hoyt Ergle when he lost both legs, including the hip joints. He was a man only to the bottom of his torso, but he never lost his head, his heart or his soul.

Despite his lack of legs, this hearty, courageous sportsman who grew up in the tiny hamlet of Island Grove in central Florida, continued his avid fishing and frog-gigging life right up until his natural, peaceful death in 1988.

By his own testimony, he cheated death at least eight times and was pushing cats for life expectancy.

His troubles began on July 1, 1958, when he was leading a team of law enforcement officers practicing for a pistol-shooting contest at Fort Lauderdale. He was a lieutenant and in charge of the group from a Florida correctional institution that was entered in the State Peace Officers' competition at their annual convention. The team went to a pistol range to practice prior to the championship tournament.

One of the officers on the team attempted to make a fast crossdraw, snatching a .45 from his holster. It was a clumsy maneuver. The pistol went off, and the only bullet fired that afternoon lodged in Ergle's back, severing his spinal cord. He fell face down in the dirt, paralyzed. Before he passed out, he directed the other officers in his own emergency treatment. Then he was rushed to a hospital in Sebring where he lost consciousness. Ironically, the bullet was made by Hoyt's own hands. Hoyt later half-jokingly talked about that irony and the accident.

"As range officer in charge of the arsenal and pistol range at the Avon Park Correctional Center, I made the ammunition for the target shooting meets. I made the very bullet that crippled me. I just happened to be in the wrong place at that particular moment, and fate took its toll. What a pity I couldn't have made a boo-boo and turned out a faulty cartridge that one time!"

Six days after being shot he regained consciousness, unable to move below his waist. His arms were black and blue from transfusions and pain-killing drug shots. He knew that he would never walk again, but was thankful to be alive and to have all his limbs.

Hoyt was not to enjoy even those luxuries for long, however. Six years after the accident, he developed an infection called osteomyelitis. One leg was amputated, but the infection continued to spread. All the best efforts of University of Florida medical experts to save his other leg were in vain. Surgeons took his remaining leg and the amputated stump, including both hip joints. He was left with a head, arms and trunk. But his spirit and determination were what marked him.

A lesser man might have hated the world and his lowly position in it, holing up in a nursing home. Not Hoyt Ergle. He was just beginning to live.

Able to pull on a pair of overalls and pin up the flapping legs, Ergle sat in a padded, circular frame or in his wheelchair and continued to live alone, doing his own cooking and driving his camper van with custom hand controls.

But he did more than that. All of his life he had been a devout fisherman and hunter. The outdoor world was his life. He would keep on enjoying it. He was determined to keep right on enjoying those beloved sports.

He had to have a little help getting into his tiny stumpbumper fishing boat where he sat in a five-gallon bucket with padding around the top. From that position, he could pull the crank rope on his 20-horsepower Mercury and start and steer it himself. His arms remained powerful.

"I was always a loner, and the best times of my life before and after I lost my legs were when I was fishing or hunting frogs by myself on Orange or Lochloosa lakes," Ergle testified. Frogging was number one on his recreation agenda.

A dozen years after he lost his legs, having stalked largemouth

bass since he was a teenager, Ergle caught his first 10-pound bass. He was so thrilled that he quit for the day, carried his fish to the taxidermist, and hung it proudly in his humble home at Island Grove. He always pointed it out to visitors, noting that he had landed the trophy fish after he lost his legs and while fishing from a boat. Not many paraplegics ever caught a 10-pound bass while fishing alone on a big lake.

Hoyt liked to tell the story:

"I was fishing a frog-spotted Dalton Special. On my second cast, I twitched that old topwater twice, and the big lunker exploded. Man, I felt like minnows were flouncing in my veins! But I got him to the boat and in the net."

One of Hoyt's eight close brushes with death came a few months after his amputations when he and a friend were setting a trotline in a pasture pond on his uncle's farm. He was sitting in his wheelchair in the bow of a narrow johnboat. He and his partner leaned the same way while baiting the trotline hooks, and he toppled over the side with his wheelchair into the eight-foot deep water. He scrambled up and down in the water three times before his friend grasped his flailing arms and hauled him over the side. It was a close call.

Frog-gigging at night from an airboat was Hoyt's first love. He liked that adventure before his accident and surgery and afterward more than any other. It was while pursuing this favorite pastime early one June evening that it happened. He rammed his airboat into a sharp limb that was barely submerged off Allen's Point in Lake Lochloosa. He had gigged here several times for small leopard and big bull frogs since becoming a paraplegic, always without incident. It was a pleasant experience for an astute outdoorsman. Not so that fateful night when the limb poked a fist-sized hole in the airboat hull. An airboat sinks mighty fast without air in its pontoons. Hoyt recalls the evening:

"I was just off the shoreline when I ruptured the pontoon. I could have pulled up on the hill and spent the night but I wanted to gig some more frogs. Luckily, some friends who were gigging in the same area came by. I told them about the hole in my boat and they volunteered to fix it so I could keep on frogging. There was no way I could get to the hole to plug it. I apologized for troubling them.

"They rammed a big piece of plastic bag in the hole and figured that would hold the boat until morning. I thanked them and kept on looking for frogs for an hour or more. Then I noticed I was getting lower in the water. The plastic plug had come out. I was sinking. I had moved out beyond the spatterdock lily line, well off from the shore and into deep water. I had to do something fast.

"I cranked the noisy old airplane engine, and headed for Cross Creek. But I was so heavy in the water that I could barely move. I figured my time was up. Luckily, I made it into the creek and saw the private landing. I got as far up the ramp as my motor would push me just as the boat gave up the ghost and went down. Fortunately, I was up on the ramp far enough so the boat couldn't completely sink. I looked down at the deck. If I had had any feet, they would have been wet. The water was two feet over the airboat deck. I yelled for help, and some tourists from close by helped me off the boat and took me home. That was the eighth of my close calls from the grim reaper."

The rest of his close calls came during dozens of painful surgical procedures after which he said survival seemed worse than death. His great desire and courage to live kept him active and enthusiastic until kidney failure claimed him at Christmas-time in a Tampa hospital in 1988.

Happiness is the state of being that most humans strive for. Often it is just beyond their grasp. They never quite catch up with it. Hoyt Ergle lived courageously one day at a time with faith and hope. During most of his 60 years, he was a cripple; a pitiful cripple many would say, but his life refutes that. His love for the outdoors and regular, successful fishing experiences kept him happy.

"I don't have to catch fish to have a good time," he said a few weeks before his nine lives gave out. Just to be out there casting a plug in another tiny nook where a big, hungry bass may be hiding out is enjoyment enough for me."

What an example he set! He will not soon be forgotten.

Saltwater
Adventures

18

Death Stalks
A Marlin Angler

by Donna Claus

There were three of us aboard the *Karma*, a 26-foot sportfishing boat out of Kona, Hawaii, and we were scrambling to boat a giant, gaffed blue marlin. The air was filled with showering seawater, shouting voices and a general uproar, as if the unfolding drama was turning our whole world upside down.

I was pulling on the leader with all my might, when Capt. Glen Van Valin leaned out to stick the great fish with the wide hook of the flying gaff. My husband Paul, exhausted from pumping and winding on this indefatigable beast for nearly three hours, was anguishing in the fighting chair. As the marlin felt the steel of the flying gaff sink solidly into his broad flank, he thrashed his wide tail and sent geysers of water flying in every direction. Pandemonium reigned.

A split second later it was as if some unseen curtain dropped on Act I of our lives. Act II was straight out of the Twilight Zone—instead of three of us aboard the *Karma*, there were suddenly only two. The crammed fight ring that was the cockpit moments ago was suddenly *empty*.

Gone were the engine cover and the fighting chair. Gone were the rod and reel—and Paul. Not even my husband's hat remained. All I could see in the empty cockpit was the now-exposed engine, and all I could hear was my own labored breathing and the steady hum of the rotating belts of the engine.

Where the water alongside the boat had been whipped to foam

an instant earlier, now only gentle ripples spread slowly over the mirror-slick surface of the mile-deep Pacific. And the ear-rending pandemonium of scant seconds before was suddenly replaced by deathly silence.

My husband had disappeared before my eyes—as if he had never existed on that boat that fateful day—as if there had been no fishing trip, and no three-hour battle with a giant marlin.

Let me start at the beginning. Paul and I own a fly-in lodge in Alaska, but in the winter we take a cue from the birds and migrate to a warmer climate. For many years now we have been spending our winters in Hawaii, where we can rest from the rigors of Alaskan outfitting and relax in the sun. Paul spends much of the time teaching scuba diving, and often guides groups on sightseeing excursions beneath the blue Hawaiian waters. In our leisure time we like to fish.

Glen also guides out of Alaska in the summer, and like us, prefers to spend his winters in Hawaii where he charters a 26-foot fishing boat out of Kailua-Kona Harbor. When Glen isn't booked, Paul and I frequently join him for a day of marlin fishing. Most of the time we spend the entire day chatting and relaxing and watching for hours on end as our live baits swim undisturbed behind the boat.

One day in particular was to break that peaceful pattern. It dawned clear and calm, as do most days in Hawaii. We pulled out of Kailua Harbor early to avoid the crush of charter boats that would soon follow and arrived at the fish buoy as the sun peeked above the volcanoes to the east. We immediately began to fish for baits, and in no time, feisty skipjack tuna (called aku here in Hawaii) were attacking our little trolled lures. Glen gently cradled the first one aboard in a wet towel and deftly bridled it to a large marlin hook. Within seconds he dropped the lively bait back into the water and began to let out line.

I took over the helm while Paul donned a large, ill-fitting, fullback harness "in preparation for fighting a blue marlin." We laughed at his optimism—our previous expeditions with Glen had been pleasant days in Paradise, but had not produced so much as a single strike.

Suddenly, as Glen was letting out the baited line, it picked up speed. He hollered, "Something's picked up the aku!"

Paul hadn't even had time to properly adjust the straps on the harness, when he grabbed the rod from Glen, settled into the fighting chair, and set the hook.

Glen reeled off a litany of instructions as we prepared to do battle with the hefty blue marlin that was now leaping clear of the water 200 yards behind the boat.

We couldn't believe we had actually hooked a marlin, but quickly responded to Glen's instructions. Paul clipped his harness straps to the harness lugs of the big reel, and buckled himself into the fighting chair itself with automobile-style seat belts, in order to gain additional leverage.

The pedestal of the fighting chair was bolted to the engine cover, which in turn was bolted to the cockpit decking. The chair was situated in the center of the cockpit, close enough to the stern covering board to allow the angler to use it as a footrest. Paul planted both feet against the covering board, and as soon as the fish stopped jumping, began the laborious task of pumping the gi-

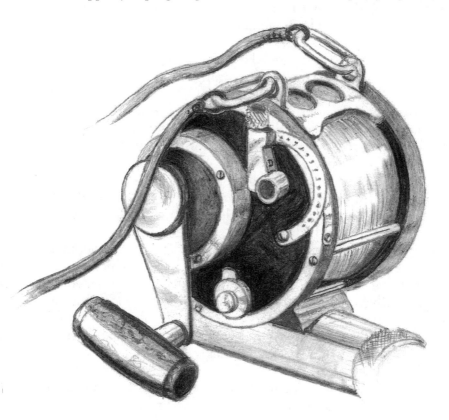

ant billfish back toward the boat.

He soon developed a rhythm, hauling back hard with a full bend on the big rod to regain line, then cranking precious inches of the 80-pound test monofilament back onto the reel as he leaned forward once again to repeat the process.

The fish never showed itself again after the initial series of jumps, and remained deep, conserving its energy. The fight became a tedious, tiring tug-of-war, and as the sun rose higher above the mountains, the tedium was compounded by rising temperatures. The excitement of the hookup had long since faded. We watched Paul sweat and strain in exhausted silence in the big fighting chair. One hour passed, then two.

At last, Paul managed to work the fish close to the boat. We watched in awe as the marlin flashed brilliant blue in the sunlight, but the image only lasted for an instant. The fish turned and once again raced off against the heavy drag. In that brief moment, however, we could see that this was *not* a 300-pound fish as we first thought. It appeared to weigh 800 pounds, perhaps more.

Paul groaned and simply held on, as he watched hard-won line melt once again from the reel. He asked for a cold drink, then resumed the long slow process of regaining the lost line yet another time.

Glen wanted this fish every bit as much as Paul did. He began to talk strategy now, and outlined the preparations necessary for landing such an enormous fish. After rooting around in the cuddy cabin, he emerged with a 10-foot, .44 caliber bang stick, and slipped a round into it. Although the use of guns or bang sticks is not allowed by International Game Fish Association (IGFA) rules, he didn't care at this point. He didn't want to lose this fish.

He ran through the battle plan. My role was to man the helm the next time Paul worked the fish close to the boat. We would try to maneuver the marlin alongside the cockpit, at which point I would leave the helm to help wire the fish. Once Glen killed the marlin with the bang stick, Paul was to quickly unbuckle himself from both the chair and the harness, and help haul the fish aboard. Once dispatched, the fish would become dead weight and sink to the bottom if we didn't secure it quickly.

The plan sounded perfect. It even worked perfectly—up to a point. Paul strained and pumped, and pumped and reeled until the giant fish lay alongside the boat. Its head was lined up around midship, and its tail extended four or five feet beyond the stern.

My heart almost stopped as I grabbed the wire leader and pulled the fish closer to the side of the boat using every ounce of strength I could muster. Glen stretched to nail the fish in the head with the bang stick, but just as he was about to thrust, the fish panicked and took off into the depths once more.

Again, Paul had to manhandle his adversary back to the boat. While he was agonizing in the fighting chair, Glen rooted through the cuddy cabin and emerged this time with a 6-inch flying gaff.

Glen knew that once he stuck the fish with the gaff, and the gaff-head pulled free of the handle, no deck cleat in the world could stand the strain of a giant fish at the end of the rope, so he secured the rope to the pedestal of the fighting chair.

The reason big game anglers traditionally tie their flying gaff ropes around the pedestal is because pedestals are always secured by heavy bolts to the deck. In some sportfishing cruisers a second post is installed beneath the decking and anchored to the keel, to add further strength to the pedestal attachment. Our chair, however, was only bolted to the engine hatch, although the hatch was securely bolted to the deck itself.

This time we were ready, and we manned our positions as Paul again brought the marlin alongside the boat. I leaped from the helm, braced myself against the inside of the gunnel, wrapped the leader wire around my gloved hand, and hauled back hard. As I pulled with all my strength, I watched Glen drop the head of the flying gaff beneath the enormous, thrashing fish, and pull up hard with both hands. He sank the stainless steel hook of the flying gaff deep, where it would surely hold.

Suddenly, our world exploded. I felt myself being yanked forward, and reached with one hand to grab the bench seat at the helm. It tore loose, but I managed to pull the glove from my other hand and release the wire before being pulled overboard.

The marlin charged away from the boat until it came to the end of the flying-gaff rope. The steel gaff head held fast in the marlin's flank, and the giant fish continued its charge beyond the length of the rope. With a great wrenching noise, the engine-hatch bolts ripped loose of the deck, and angler, chair and engine hatch flew out of the cockpit. As the hatch cover and chair flew past Glen, it smashed into him, knocking him to the deck.

Dazed, I stood up and looked aft. Everything was gone. In the space formerly occupied by the fighting chair, with its pedestal anchored firmly to the broad engine hatch and the cockpit deck, there was only a gaping hole—and the engine. Only the hum of its rotating belts broke the deathly silence. Where moments before there had been shouts of frantic activity, in the space of a heartbeat, pandemonium had turned to awesome stillness.

I began to scream hysterically for Paul as I stumbled around the hole in the cockpit in a daze. I peered into the cobalt depths and searched the empty ocean around the boat. There was no visible sign that anything had happened.

The silence was palpable, and I was convinced that I had suddenly become a widow. Seconds seemed like minutes.

I have no idea how long it was before I heard Paul's voice scream out, "I'm alive! I'm alive! Praise the Lord, I'm alive!" I looked in the direction of the shout and saw my husband bobbing at the surface.

Rejoicing, I glanced at Glen—and gasped. His face was covered with blood, and as I stooped to pick up a towel, I could see where our footprints had painted the deck blood-red.

I wrapped Glen's head in the towel, and turned to help Paul. He clambered aboard the *Karma* and tried to stand, only to fall forward onto the deck. His sense of balance was gone.

As Glen manned the helm and turned the *Karma* toward home, Paul and I looked into each other's faces in shock, and alternately laughed and fell silent. Now that we were both safe in the boat and heading for shore, the image of what had just transpired seemed unreal. We felt as if we had just awakened from a nightmare, but our senses had not yet sorted out the details. Had all this really happened?

By the time we reached shore, we had begun to regain our senses, and on the way to the hospital, Paul recounted all he could remember of the ordeal.

"The minute I hit the water, I knew that I was in a fight for my very life. I was being towed through the water at a terrific rate of speed. It felt as if I had failed to let go of the tow rope after a fall on water skis. The rush of the water was so great that it was all I could do to pull my arms in front of me and try to get out of the harness that connected me to this runaway freight train.

"I thought of you and of our dangerous lifestyle in Alaska—

and of eternity. I knew I was going to die, and the thought that this was a stupid way to go flashed through my mind. But I remember making a conscious decision to fight, no matter what the odds.

"As I was being dragged downward, the rod jerked in spasms against the harness straps. I managed to slip one arm out of the harness. If I could just get rid of the harness, I thought, I would be free. The thought that you or Glen might be entangled with me flashed through my mind, and I prayed that you were not.

"Then, just as suddenly as I had been yanked into the water, both arms came loose. I was free of the harness and the whipping rod. I knew I had to get to the surface, and fast.

"Once I regained my orientation, I looked up and saw light. My lungs felt as if they would burst, and I knew that I had to swim hard to make it to the surface.

"It was a long way to the top—80 to 100 feet, at least, and I knew I was running a risk of blackout from oxygen depletion.

Thank God for my diver's training, and my ability to hold my breath far longer than the average person.

"Suddenly, I was able to make out the light-colored form of the boat about 30 feet above me. I still had enough presence of mind to realize that I must swim to one side to avoid coming up directly beneath it. When I made it to the surface, I just gasped. My lungs were burning and I felt like passing out. All I could think of was, 'I'm alive!'"

The doctor could scarcely believe our incredible story. He sewed 11 stitches in Glen's head and taped up several ribs, which had been broken when the hatch and chair smashed into him as they flew overboard. Paul's ears were also in poor shape from the collision, but at least the drums weren't punctured. The doctor gave him a prescription for antibiotics and released him. Within days, he was leading scuba diving trips once again.

As soon as Glen's boat was repaired, we resumed our occasional fishing trips with him, but we never saw another marlin.

Sometimes, my mind flashes back to that day when a curtain fell, and part of my world disappeared in an instant. And I remember seeing the great blue beast that almost made me a widow.

19

The Magic Marlin

by Don Mann

When I was a naive youth, I thought the oft-repeated line, "A rose is a rose, is a rose," was merely a simplistic statement of the obvious, rather than an eloquent definition of indefinable beauty.

Several years ago, several miles off the Pacific coast of Panama, I might have asked whether a rose was indeed a rose at all.

Or, at the very least, whether a great, leaping black marlin was a black marlin at all. Without delving into epistemological debate, I'm simply reporting what I saw with my own eyes. I witnessed a magnificent black marlin transform itself into an ugly white-tipped shark—but let me start at the beginning.

Mark Yount, a young marine artist from West Palm Beach, Florida, and I were live-baiting over Hannibal Bank, a famed seamount off the Pacific coast of Panama noted for its incredible springtime billfishing.

Our target was black marlin, and indeed I had landed a hefty 300-pounder earlier in the day. Now, it was Mark's turn on the rod. I caught a feisty, eight-pound skipjack tuna on a feather jig, and our captain deftly rigged it to a 12/0 marlin hook with a Dacron bridle and returned him to the water in a matter of seconds. Then, by alternately kicking the engine in and out of gear, we slowly power-drifted the lively little tuna behind our small, center-console skiff.

The Pacific was greasy-slick that day, and the cable leader barely rippled the surface as it slowly sliced through the water.

Mark's live bait swam obediently behind our boat as the captain turned the boat in large, lazy circles over the bait-rich hump far below.

Live-baiting for giant billfish is one of the most relaxing forms of fishing and yet the most tension-filled. On the one hand, the stillness of the scene and the low growl of the idling diesel are disarmingly peaceful. The faint ripples spreading before the boat and the bait create wavy reflections of occasional clouds on the mirror surface of the sea. Such tranquility encourages dozing.

On the other hand, the tuna, with its mobility handicapped by a tether of steel-stranded cable, must undoubtedly feel anything but serene. Although able to swim behind the boat in apparently normal fashion, he is actually a gladiator about to enter an arena full of lions—and you get the feeling that he must be aware of that role. Despite the apparent serenity above the surface of the sea, the tuna's anxiety does wear on the angler above who knows that the tuna is nerve-rackingly sensitive to any sign of an approaching predator. The subtle tension of impending pandemonium can be downright palpable.

Sure enough, within minutes the tuna came alive and quivered nervously off to one side of the boat. All aboard experienced a sudden surge of adrenalin as we watched the steel leader slice faster and faster through the water. We knew what was about to happen, although the still-smooth Pacific offered no clue to the presence of the unseen predator that had obviously terrified the swimming bait.

Seconds later, the water erupted where the tuna had been, and the line sizzled beyond the growing circle of ripples where something, still unseen, had consumed Mark's hapless bait. The line no longer cut through the water like a sharp knife—now it left a perceptible wake. Mark freespooled the big reel and watched his line disappear at a frightening rate. Moments later he gathered his faculties and shoved the drag lever of the big gold reel forward to the strike position. When the line came tight, he hauled back on the rod with all the strength he could muster to set the oversize hook.

A quarter-ton black marlin burst into the air at the feel of the steel barb, showering water like a cloudburst. The broad-shouldered fish landed, then greyhounded away from the boat, leaping into the air again and again like a porpoise, leaving behind great foaming puddles with each successive splashdown.

Finally, several hundred yards behind the boat, the giant marlin made one final leap, reaching still higher than before. This time he thrust his mammoth bulk completely out of the water, tail and all, as if he thought the hand of God would snatch away the offending hook if he leapt high enough. And then, just as suddenly, he disappeared beneath the surface of the no-longer-tranquil Pacific. The tug-of-war began.

For 45 minutes Mark struggled with the giant weight on the other end of his line. Little by little he pumped and reeled, gaining line turn by turn against the powerful fish that was dogging it far below the boat. Sweat poured down his reddened face and into his eyes—fighting monstrous fish under the hot tropical sun of Panama is not a task for the faint-hearted.

We shouted encouragement and emptied the contents of the ice chest over his head when he protested that he couldn't hold on much longer. But hold on he did, pumping and winding until at long last, the double line, then the swivel clip cleared the surface of the water. The captain stretched for the heavy cable leader with gloved hands to haul in Mark's trophy marlin. None of us were prepared for the apparition that rose from below.

An enormous oceanic whitetip shark, the marlin hook firmly embedded in the corner of his mouth, thrashed the water white beside the boat. Its great jaws snapped audibly at the cable, while we stared in stunned disbelief. Then, as if prompted by some unseen conductor, the three of us shouted in unison, "Where's the marlin?"

The captain hastily snipped the leader, far from the snapping jaws of the angry fish on the other end of Mark's line. Confused and shaken, we tried to figure out what had happened to the marlin that had consumed Mark's bait an hour earlier. After all, we had seen it with our own eyes. We had all watched a monstrous black marlin, apparently hooked solidly, leap repeatedly away from our boat.

Mark, always the scientifically-oriented realist, theorized that the big black marlin threw the hook with the tuna still secured by its Dacron bridle. When it made its final leap far from the boat, the tuna must have dropped to the water hidden from our view by the geyser created by the leaping fish. Incredibly, Mark reasoned, the shark must have been swimming directly beneath the leaping marlin and gobbled the hooked bait after it landed on his head.

Mark's imagined reenactment became still more complicated. The tension on the line, which never went slack, must have remained constant because of the water pressure created by a belly in the line.

It was the only plausible explanation for a black marlin to have turned into a whitetip shark.

Whatever the scenario, we all learned an important lesson: It may not always be true that a marlin is a marlin, is a marlin.

=20=

My Last Voyage On
The Finalista

= by Mike Katz =

When I embarked on a fishing trip on the *Finalista*, the first clue that it would be a star-crossed voyage on a jinxed fishing boat came when the generators quit on the first day out. It happened at lunchtime in broad daylight, so no one thought much about the lack of power at the time. However, when the captain said "No problem—it'll be fixed in a jiffy," I had a premonition.

Some hours later, when it was time once again to head for the galley for dinner, it looked as if the problem was solved. A hot meal was waiting for us. We soon discovered, however, that our hot meal did not mean we had power. The cook stoves were butane-powered and we still had plenty of butane. The word quickly spread that the generators had defied all efforts to get them going again. Nothing that required electricity worked—neither the lights or the freezer units. My premonition about the boat was fast becoming a reality.

After dinner we groped our way out of the galley, shuffled carefully down the inky-dark companionway to our cabins and stumbled into the sack. Things were not going well.

Whenever you book a long-range fishing trip out of San Diego into Mexican waters, you are gambling on good fishing. You recognize the realities of the sport—the fishing may be great, or it may be lousy. Seldom do you consider that you're also gambling on the vessel itself. It was beginning to look as if we had put our money on a real loser.

Our trip had begun like any other fishing foray. When my old fishing buddy Cees called me some weeks earlier, he said that he, Frank and Charlie were planning to book a five-day albacore trip down the Baja coast. We would be fishing on a boat called the *Finalista* out of San Diego. She was not the boat we usually chartered, but the latest reports indicated that the *Finalista* had been bringing in good catches..

Departure date was set for September 8, so I made arrangements for someone to mind our store (Mike's Bait and Tackle) while I was gone. When I arrived the morning of the 8th to pick up Charlie, Cecil was already there with his camper, which he had completely emptied. Ever the optimist, he had cleaned it out to hold all the iced-down fish he expected the four of us to catch during the trip.

We met at the waterfront parking lot, checked in, and stowed our gear aboard the *Finalista*. I remembered to check with the skipper to be sure he had our Mexican fishing licenses. On a previous trip they had been forgotten and we had to return to port to get them. That's one thing you take dead seriously—Mexican officials can be sticklers about licenses. They've even been known to nail non-fishing boaters for cruising without fishing licenses just because there were emergency hooks and lines stowed in the vessel's life rafts. The hooks qualified as sportfishing tackle and licenses were required. You don't fool around with an attitude like that.

We sailed out of San Diego harbor early in the evening. The weather was perfect. Knowing that we would have to get up early to catch bait, we hit the sack immediately.

At 3 a.m. we dropped anchor off Guadalupe Island and all hands turned out to jig for mackerel to fill the live-bait wells. By breakfast time we were still catching bait, so we had to eat and fish in shifts until 7:30 a.m., when the bait wells were full. Chomping at the bit for some action, we headed south along the Baja coast.

At 10 a.m. both outriggers turned loose and a whole lot of shouting and running around the decks signaled that we were in a large school of albacore.

I grabbed my light rod spooled with 40-pound test line from the rack and scrambled for the livewell. The next 45 minutes were filled with the excitement we had all come aboard to enjoy. Deck hands were running back and forth along the railings, gaffing and

tagging fish. The school held albacore between 15 and 25 pounds, nice fat beauties that gave you a dogged fight. By the time I landed my fifth fish, my arms were beginning to feel the strain, but when you're into albacore, you can't think about things like that. Cecil landed seven fish, while Frank, Charlie and I each boated five.

As fast as the frenzy began—it ended. In a very short period of time, 20 anglers had boated about 100 albacore. Nearly a ton of tuna was stowed in the refrigerated hold of the *Finalista*.

We continued down the coast, taking turns trolling from the stern. For that I switched to my heavy rod and Penn Senator 12/0 reel spooled with 80-pound test monofilament line. I fished a yellow and white Tuna Clone when it was my turn at the railing.

I had no success so when my turn was up I headed for the galley and lunch. That was when the generators quit, and I had the ominous feeling that our troubles were just beginning.

After lunch, when it was my turn to troll once again, the boat slowed down drastically. One of the two diesel engines had simply quit. The captain announced a short time later that it looked as if it couldn't be fixed, but "Not to worry, we can do just fine on one engine."

Sure, just fine. Our trolling speed was not up to what I would have preferred for tuna, but we grudgingly accepted what we couldn't change.

That evening we enjoyed a hot dinner cooked on butane stoves—at least *they* worked. We sat around the galley telling lies until dark, then groped our way to our cabins and hit the sack. We slept like the dead. With one engine and the generators gone, what else could possibly happen to us?

At 2 a.m. I found out. Our star-crossed vessel still held a few more surprises.

Cecil first noticed it. He bolted upright in his bunk and said, "What's that awful smell?"

I felt around in the pitch dark for my rubber boots, put them on and went topside. Our cabin was at the very foot of the ladder, and just across the passageway from the top of the ladder were the heads. They were pouring out their contents, which flowed down the ladder like a waterfall into our cabin below. We could handle a lack of power, but this was something else again.

I sloshed my way to the wheelhouse and reported the problem to the captain. He sent a crewman down to take a look. No matter how well he fixed the mechanical problem, all the air freshener in the world could not make the area below deck endurable for the rest of our journey.

When I reported the overflowing heads, the captain told me that he was returning to San Diego. I guess he figured he'd have a mutiny on his hands pretty soon and wanted to make port before all hands got ugly—or before he lost the other engine.

But first, he announced, he was going to put in at Cedros Island to get ice for the fish in the hold. With the generators out the refrigeration units weren't working, and the combination of a ton

of spoiled tuna and the raw sewage that filled the lower companionway would have guaranteed a rebellion.

When we arrived at Cedros Island about six in the morning, the place was a shambles. A chubasco had hit the area the night before. These sudden and very powerful windstorms occasionally occur in September around the area of the Baja peninsula. This one must have been a beauty. The pier looked like a pile of matchsticks and debris was scattered around the entire area.

Since foreign registry vessels should never tie up or allow passengers to go ashore without permission, especially in Mexico, we stood off shore, looking for signs of life. We saw no one, so we pulled close to the remains of the pier and dropped off one of our Mexican crewmen to look for the port captain. Then we pulled back out and waited.

An hour later, we saw the crewman waving to us from the end of the pier. When we picked him up, he reported that the port captain wanted five dozen eggs and three bottles of whiskey before he would discuss our needs. We pulled back away from the dock and waited.

A short time later, we saw three men picking their way over the broken planking of the pier. One of them had to be the port captain. He wore a navy blue cap with crossed anchors above the bill, a grimy T-shirt that was partially hidden under an olive-colored shirt buttoned once across his bloated belly, baggy shorts that stopped short of his knobby knees, no socks and a pair of scruffy shoes that looked like thrift store rejects. You couldn't have imagined a more perfect Mexican port captain.

We pulled up close to the end of the pier and passed the eggs and whiskey over to him in a long-handled dip net. He took the items without a word, handed them to his two assistants, shouted "¡No tenemos hielo!"—then turned and walked away. "We have no ice!"

We were batting 1000. I figured I might as well salvage whatever I could from the trip, so I trolled on the way back to San Diego. I got a hellaceous hit and shouted to the skipper to slow down so that I could land whatever it was.

Fortunately, it wasn't a large tuna—but a mahi-mahi. The captain yelled back, "I'm not slowing down. Bounce the S.O.B." Luckily, I bounced the fish onto the deck, and gave it to a dejected young man I'd met on the boat. He had saved a long time for this

My Last Voyage On The Finalista   141

trip and it hadn't turned out as he'd dreamed it would.

Once ashore, we discovered that *all* wasn't lost. Most of the albacore had survived unspoiled in the refrigerated hold. We swapped our fish for canned albacore at the local cannery and headed for the booking office.

Evidently, we out-hollered them. They gave us free passes for a future trip on the *Finalista*. Several weeks later our dilemma over whether we really wanted to fish aboard that particular vessel ever again was solved.

On her very next voyage the *Finalista* caught fire and burned to the waterline. Star-crossed, indeed!

21

The Billfish Deadline

by Don Mann

"There's a fish on here!" I shouted, trying to make myself heard over a wall of raw water that crashed over the transom out of the Caribbean night and swept into the cockpit.

The 80-pound-class rod bent into a deep bow and I pumped, feeling the strain of a fish 500 feet below. The depression that had gripped me for the past two hours while we bobbed on the rough surface of the Caribbean Sea off Venezuela disappeared in a wave of hope.

As we backed down that night into the crashing seas, under constant hosing by near gale-force winds, I felt certain it was a broadbill that had taken my squid bait far below. "It *has* to be a broadbill," I thought to myself, as I strained in the big fighting chair against my as-yet-unseen quarry.

The reason for my even being out on such a night was to catch a broadbill—and end a year-long odyssey, my quest to catch all nine of the world's billfish recognized by the International Game Fish Association, the arbiter of fishing catches and records throughout the world. Nobody had ever done it before—much less within the short span of 12 months.

Now, with eight of the nine fish under my belt, there were only three weeks left on my 12-month timetable—and I needed a broadbill swordfish. I was fighting not only a great fish, but also a nerve-racking deadline.

Let me start at the beginning, on a much calmer day off the

Lower Keys of Florida, a hot but significant day.

The date was June 28. We were trolling for blue marlin 18 miles off Big Pine Key with thunderstorms surrounding us and dictating our trolling pattern. We zig-zagged about the ocean, seeking out areas that were clear of dark clouds and booming thunder.

The only action all morning was provided by one obviously lost giant barracuda that smacked a trolled marlin lure in 700 feet of water.

The temperature climbed all day. By one in the afternoon, it was near 90 degrees and the humidity was pushing what felt like 100 percent. By two o'clock I was fighting back heavy eyelids while trying to maintain my watch on our skipping lures from my perch atop the rocket launcher.

Suddenly, the right outrigger clip released its line with an authoritative "crack"—not the light snap that sounds when the lure snags seaweed and pulls the line from the clip. As I grabbed the rod from the holder, I startled our skipper, Richard Price, with a scream, "Punch it!" He immediately rammed the throttles forward while I hauled back hard and repeatedly on the rod. Whatever had nailed the little pink-and-blue lure was not about to throw the two 8/0 stainless hooks if I could help it.

"It's a little bitty blue," Richard shouted from his vantage point in the 25-foot Mako's tower.

"Too small and skinny," I shouted back. "It looks like a white." I admitted to myself that it really looked like another 'cuda—long and slender and silver—but I thought that I had seen a bill during the first twisting leap.

As if reading my mind, Richard assured Roger Baker and me that he had certainly seen a bill. Roger cleared the other lines as I pumped and reeled from a standing position. Another jump, still far from the boat, confirmed that whatever was on the other end of my line was a long, slender billfish. "It must be a skinny white," I hollered, with less than firm conviction.

In a matter of minutes, the fish was alongside the boat. It was indeed very long for its girth, and an electric blue color from one end to the other. The bill was slender, but disproportionately short, and much too slender at the tip to have been broken off. The leading end of the dorsal fin looked slightly rounded, much like that of a white marlin. The pectoral fins were exceptionally long, but pointed, not rounded at the end like most whites. As a

Complete Angler's Library

multitude of questions raced through my head, I grabbed the heavy monofilament leader with my left hand and pulled the fish up the side of the boat.

"It's a spearfish!" I yelled when the identity of this skinny apparition finally registered. The fin was indeed like no other. It reached nearly to the tail, yet was uniformly short. A spearfish, the rarest of all billfish. I had never before seen one, much less hooked one, but I'd seen many pictures.

Roger managed a grip on the one-hand-long bill and swung the catch aboard. Richard had laid aside the tagging stick as soon as we identified the fish. He knew I was keeping this one—it was a once-in-a-lifetime catch.

We were heading back to the marina to weigh my trophy (it later tipped the scales at 26 pounds, 4 ounces), when I had a brainstorm. The idea had been in there a long time, actually. It was only given new life by the catch that lay in the cockpit before me. Several years earlier I had toyed with the idea of trying to land a representative specimen of each of the world's billfish within a one-year period. That year I had taken two black marlin and a Pacific sailfish in the Pacific waters of Panama in April, and added two Atlantic blue marlin in St. Thomas in July. On a November trip to Ecuador, a few striped marlin joined the list. But then the plan fizzled. Two unsuccessful attempts at a broadbill swordfish off Miami netted me a pulled hook on a beauty—and several immense Cuban night sharks. A subsequent pulled hook attempt to rack up a white marlin off Chub Cay in the Bahamas put the final damper on the idea.

Now, however, the dream was "on" once again—and tallying *every* one of the nine species within a 12-month period was distinctly possible. If I were to begin counting the 12-month period several months earlier, I would already have half of the nine fish needed to complete the Royal Slam. I had already scored billfish in Panama back in March and in Key West in May. What if I started counting in March?

The Panama trip had been a spectacular adventure. In a single morning, fishing alone with Capt. Geronimo in a 23-foot center console open fisherman, I had caught three black marlin and a Pacific blue marlin, a one-angler, one-day record for the camp that stood until it closed. We even came in early for lunch. The date was March 9. That would be the starting date for my self-imposed, one-year, catch-all-nine deadline.

Two days later, on March 11, I had caught a Pacific sailfish. Within the first three days of my arbitrary year I already had three of the nine species I needed. Two months later, on May 12, I had been fishing with my buddy Richard Price off Key West, Florida and hooked into an Atlantic blue marlin. I released the fish, which weighed an estimated 175 pounds.

And now, here it was June 28, and I had the spearfish—and a total of five of the nine species under my belt. When we hit shore, after weighing the spearfish and arranging to have it mounted Richard, Roger, and I retired to a local watering hole to savor our catch—and lay plans for my brainstorm.

I had eight full months left in which to catch the four other billfish. The remaining four constituted quite a challenge, however. I still needed a striped marlin, a Pacific fish; both a white marlin and an Atlantic sailfish, both Atlantic fish; and a broadbill swordfish, which theoretically could be found in either ocean.

I figured I could get a striped marlin at Salinas, Ecuador, in the fall, so that one should be easy. I reasoned that the Atlantic sailfish should also be easy—they run in substantial numbers close to my Miami home in the winter.

The white could be a problem. There are relatively rare catches off South Florida, and the nearby fisheries at Bimini and Chub Cay in the Bahamas hadn't been dependable in recent years. Ocean City, Maryland, boasted excellent white marlin fishing in the summertime. Unfortunately, I had no contacts in Maryland. I didn't even want to think about the broadbill just yet. Broadbill fisheries had been declining throughout the world in recent years under intense commercial fishing pressure. I decided to leave the swordfish for last.

The minute I got home from the Keys, I phoned my old friend Knudie Holst who runs the charter fleet out of Salinas, Ecuador, to make plans for me to come down in early October. I felt confident that my striped marlin was in the bag.

But I was still worried about finding a white. I hadn't the foggiest notion where to find a white in the summertime. In early July I called some friends at Shimano tackle for help. They provided a lead from their list of tackle testers. I called the number Shimano gave me.

It seems that Joe Judge had shipped his boat from Maryland to

The Billfish Deadline

La Guaira, Venezuela, and was flying down periodically to fish. If I could make it down when Joe wasn't using the boat, he would be happy to let me use it. I gratefully accepted his invitation and planned a trip in early September.

When I arrived in Venezuela, however, the seas were running eight to 10-feet, far too rough to fish comfortably from Joe's boat. During my four-day stay we managed to get out for two half-days of fishing. I must admit I had my shots at white marlin, but I failed to hook up with the three or four fish that inspected our rigged-ballyhoo baits. Disappointed, I returned home.

Back in Miami, I searched out the booking agent for Keen International, an organization that ran two charter boats out of La Guaira. Both of Keen's charter boats were larger than Joe Judge's, reducing the possibility of getting weathered out. I booked a one-day trip in November, after my Ecuador trip.

I knew that the October trip to Ecuador would undoubtedly be my only shot at a striped marlin, and that I'd just have to be optimistic about my chances for adding the white in November.

October finally rolled around, and Knudie Holst came through. The waters off Salinas were alive with stripes during my entire visit. Every day we saw dozens of tailing fish, surfing down the large, rolling swells of the Equatorial Current. And every day we found at least a few that were interested in our trolled ballyhoo. I not only added a striped marlin to my list, I caught four of them—and lost a giant Pacific blue marlin after a five-hour struggle. The loss of the giant blue really didn't matter—I already had my Pacific blue from Panama.

The following month, I packed up my 30-pound class rods and reels and headed for Venezuela. It was do-or-die. This would be my last chance to nail a white marlin, but this time either my skills, or my luck, improved. By 11 o'clock in the morning I found myself tied into a feisty little 50-pound white marlin. I fed him a tiny ballyhoo behind the boat, as he chased a mullet teaser right to the transom.

Once the fish was hooked and released, I heaved a huge sigh of relief and told the captain to head for home. He insisted that we might as well continue fishing, perhaps go for a Grand Slam by adding a blue and a sail. I proceeded to pull hooks on both a blue and a sail before mid-afternoon. Although a Grand Slam was not to be, it was still celebration time.

Nearly four months remained for me to catch an Atlantic sail and a broadbill. The sail would be next. I figured that catching a sail near home should be easy, since Miami lies smack in the middle of some of the world's best wintertime sailfishing.

Two day-trips to the Florida Keys in December to fish with my friend Richard Price failed to produce so much as a sailfish sighting, but on January 18th I drove down to fish out of Key West with another fishing buddy, Jerry Dixon.

Jerry guaranteed a sail—I couldn't pass up such optimism. We drifted live blue runners west of Sands Key, using spinning tackle and 16-pound test line, and within two hours of setting out our baits a hungry sail consumed my hapless runner. Fifteen action-filled minutes later, I added an Atlantic sailfish to the list.

Eight down! One to go! And less than two months left.

Where in the world could I find a broadbill? Several years earlier the East Coast of Florida was considered one of the finest broadbill fisheries in the world, but heavy commercial longline pressure had reduced the stocks to next to nothing. Still, it was close to home and worth a try.

Again, I sought out an old friend, Capt. Jim Sharp, who charters out of the Lower Keys. Caught up in the excitement of the quest, he quickly volunteered to help. He and his son and I spent a long, cold night in early February off Florida's Summerland Key monitoring deep squid baits as we drifted east in the Gulf Stream. We caught only several small sharks, and I had less than a month to go before my March 9 deadline.

In desperation, I got on the phone once again. Jerry Dunaway, the world-renowned angler from Houston, Texas, provided some advice. He had just returned from Tropic Star Lodge in Panama, where he had found perhaps the greatest concentration of broadbills anywhere in the world. But he had run into a problem in these fertile Pacific waters. It seems that hordes of giant cannibal squids were eating all of his dead-squid baits before he could drop them below the "squid layer" to the broadbills that lurked in the depths below. "They're there," Jerry said, "but it's nearly impossible to get your baits down to them.

"The only place I know of where you just might catch yourself a broadbill at this time of year would be Venezuela," he offered.

Once again, I contacted the folks at Keen International, and explained my desperate deadline. They agreed to get me out for one night of swordfishing on their 46' Bertram, the Margullia—weather permitting.

Eagerly, I packed up my heavy tackle once again, and headed for Venezuela. When I arrived, Capt. Luis Suarez was just as excited as I was. It was heartwarming to see the eager enthusiasm of both the owner, Morris Van Grieken, and his crew. However, I would only have a single night to fish, and the seas offshore looked like the French Alps. If I had been a routine charter client, there is no way they would have attempted the trip.

However, to a man, the crew agreed to give it a try when I explained that this was undoubtedly my last shot at the broadbill. It was also my last shot at doing something no one had ever done before, scoring what was later to be named a "Royal Slam" within one year. They were as excited at the prospect as I was.

That night, exhausted and drenched to the skin from constantly backing into the maelstrom to keep our deep baits straight up and down, I hooked my broadbill, a fat-as-a-sausage 90-pounds. The pressure was off. At last. With just three weeks left in my self-imposed 12-month deadline, my place in the Guinness Book of World Records was assured.

22

Fishing To Survive

by Capt. Skip Nielsen

There was a time when I thought there were only two kinds of fishing—commercial and recreational. A terrifying, two-week ordeal at sea taught me that there is yet a third kind of fishing—survival. Believe me, it's not in the same league as the other two.

I have enjoyed recreational angling all my life, and have earned my living as a charter boat captain for most of it. About 15 years ago I worked briefly as a fishing guide at the famed Costa Rica fishing camp, Bahia Pez Vela. Located on the country's northern Pacific coast facing the Gulf of Papagayo, the camp was aptly named. These waters held incredible numbers of sailfish (pez vela)—as well as marlin and assorted inshore gamefish. Each spring, stateside anglers travel in droves to this little democratic country in Central America to test their light-tackle skills against sporting gamefish. The camp is comfortable, and back then I made a comfortable living doing what I enjoyed most, fishing.

I had worked almost daily since my arrival in May, but by July bookings slacked off a bit, so I decided to take a long weekend off to be with several friends. Robbie Haid, an experienced sailor, borrowed an old sailboat left at anchor at nearby Playas del Coco by a Californian who visited infrequently. She was a 26-foot sloop-rigged, double-ended, converted whale boat with a single mast and a large tiller. She had been long neglected by her absentee owner, her engine didn't work and she had no batteries. Despite the boat's poor shape, Robbie figured she would do just fine for a short weekend jaunt.

Together with Dave Russell, an inventive boatman and long-time friend, Mark, a teen-aged acquaintance from Alaska, and my girlfriend, Joanie, we planned a fun weekend.

Twenty-seven miles northwest of the camp, and just beyond the rocky outcrops known as the Bat Islands, the long Santa Elena Peninsula juts west into the Pacific. Along that peninsula at the northwestern corner of the Gulf of Papagayo lies a beautiful beach called Playa Grande. We planned a three-day trip to this beach to relax, do a little surfing and maybe catch some roosterfish from the shore.

Before we left, we stocked up minimally for our two-night trip. We filled the boat's 20-gallon water tank, and took some potatoes and onions to go with the fish we expected to catch. We had a dozen limes, a few avocados and strangely, two quart jars of honey. I was the cook in the crowd and planned on frying fresh-caught fish over a fire on the beach.

Although the others brought their surfboards in anticipation of some excellent surfing at Playa Grande, I had a different diversion in mind. I took along one heavy flyrod, a number of large tarpon and sailfish flies, two spinning outfits spooled with 10- and 20-pound test line, and one plug outfit spooled with 15-pound test. I also brought along a bag of bucktail jigs, trolling jigs, plugs and all manner of terminal tackle. I planned on doing a lot of casting from the isolated beaches of Playa Grande and was ready for anything—but I was really hoping for a trophy roosterfish.

We got an early start, hoping to get to our destination in time to get settled well before dark. The day dawned hot, sunny and cloudless. A light breeze filled our sails.

Around 1 p.m., some 12 miles from shore, the wind suddenly died. Soon afterwards, we were shocked by the ominous sight of white water in the distance. We watched spellbound as the white-caps advanced on us, until finally we found ourselves in the midst of a howling maelstrom. Within one hour it was blowing 40 knots out of the northeast, and the high, shrill screaming of the wind became deafening.

We were caught in a viento diablo, a devil wind. These Papagayo winds are called chubascos farther north in Baja Mexico, where they occasionally spring up in September with devastating results. Here, in the dry northern province of Guanacaste in Costa Rica, however, one only expects such super-strong northerly blasts between December and April; at the very latest, May. Here it was July and we were unquestionably caught in a vicious Papagayo wind.

To make matters worse, we were being driven toward the Bat Islands. These jagged rocks, which rise like sentinels from the ocean depths off the western end of the Santa Elena Peninsula, would rip our little sailboat to pieces. By sunset, we were driven dangerously close. We thought about anchoring, but there was only 100 feet of anchor rope on board, not enough to reach bottom. We couldn't jump for it either because these waters contain a large number of enormous sharks.

With diminished options, we dropped our sails and turned southwest to ride out the storm with the wind at our backs. Our only thought at that time was to avoid the rocks of the Bat Islands.

That night the wind not only failed to let up, it increased to between 60 and 70 knots, and its high-pitched scream became deafening. Our principal concern then was to keep the boat afloat. We tried to point our bow into the wind by dragging a sea anchor from the stern. Then we tried to turn stern-to using the sea anchor at our bow. Either way, Robbie had all he could do to manhandle the large tiller and keep us from broaching before the rising swells. Our 26-foot sailboat was surfing along with the wind toward the southwest. She was pitching fore and aft and taking breakers of green water over her decks one after the other.

While Robbie fought his demons at the helm, the rest of us huddled in the little cabin, taking two-hour shifts at the bilge pump. All we had was a little hand pump, the kind you use to pump the head. By pumping frantically all through the night, we were barely able to keep ahead of the water that rose in the bilge through the seams in the bottom planking. The storm had opened us up and the sea was pouring through.

By morning the seas had assumed mountainous proportions; the waves were 20 feet high. They were made all the steeper by the fact that the wind and current were running in opposite directions. Although the current was running strongly toward the north, the gale-force winds predominated and pushed us relentlessly toward the southwest.

All day long we were in the same predicament. We couldn't let up our pumping efforts for a minute because we were taking on water from all directions. Not only was it leaking through the seams in the planking, but it was crashing over us from above.

Despite the rough seas, I broke out my fishing tackle on Saturday, between shifts at the tiller. A large school of dorado, which are well known to hang around floating debris, had taken up a station beneath our drifting boat. Six- to 8-pound schoolies readily ate my bucktails, and a trophy size bull I estimated to weigh more than 50 pounds ate a fly. I lost the big one, and remember thinking that he was probably world-record size. We would have kept him for supper anyhow.

I caught plenty of his younger brothers, however, and with the help of the bag of limes and the onions we had brought aboard, I made delicious seviche all weekend. The lime juice was acidic and, in effect, "cooked" the finely-chopped fish. We would have cooked on the galley stove, but it was out of fuel.

For the first five days the wind blew unabated. The seas remained high, and we had to use safety ropes whenever we went topside to fish or take a turn at the tiller. Our school of dorado stayed with us the entire time, so we had no trouble catching fish, but we gradually used up our small supply of vegetables. The several avocados had turned to mush by the incessant pounding the first couple of days, but we did find some old rusty canned goods below. They were without labels, so we opened up one each day for a surprise snack to share among the five of us.

During that time we didn't make any particular effort to ration our water supply, because we thought we would be rescued at any moment. On the third day we ran out of limes, however, so we no longer had any way to marinate the fish I was catching. From then on, we had to eat it raw, Sushi-style. I continued to fish, even though we had more fish than we needed, simply to pass the time between pumping and tiller shifts. We took four-hour shifts on the tiller, and continuous two-hour shifts on the little pump, round the clock.

By the fourth day it was beginning to look like we were in for a long ordeal, so we began rationing water—two glasses per day per person. Our water supply held out until early on the sixth day. Although we were getting moisture from the raw fish we were eating, it wasn't enough to truly quench a thirst.

Days four and five were filled with the monotony of our steering and pumping chores. The mountainous seas continued to hammer our little craft without letup. The strong northerly current was running against the howling winds, and there was no way we could even attempt to sail against such elements. The wind continued to drive us to the southwest.

Dave, our Mr. Fix-It, had been repairing our little pump regularly throughout the ordeal. Each time the gasket in the pump wore out, he replaced it with a piece of vinyl cut from the covers of our cushions. His inventiveness saved our skins, because if our little pump had given out, we would have lost it all.

During the first several days we saw a number of ships. We fired three flares when one passed within about a mile and a half of us, but no one saw them. We surmised that the freighters were probably on auto-pilot with no human eyes on the bridge. We heard several planes, too, but our little white boat must have been virtually invisible against the frothy white surface of the storm-whipped sea.

We even hoisted a piece of metal up the mast, hoping it would act as a radar deflector, but since the swells towered over us, nobody picked up the blip. A hand mirror failed to attract attention, as well. We were on our own, but our spirits were still good. We figured that if we were to survive, we would have to take our destiny into our own hands. We would have to try to keep body and boat together and sail home when the windstorm subsided.

Finally, Mother Nature came around. The sixth day dawned clear and calmer—both winds and seas dropped considerably. For the first time we were able to move about our little vessel, tidy up, and take stock.

As if that weren't enough good fortune, that morning we spotted a 150-pound loggerhead turtle nuzzling our sea anchor. The poor misguided creature looked as if it was trying to make love to it. Using a small homemade gaff we had brought for our "fishing trip," we managed to gaff the turtle. After slitting its throat, we butchered it on the deck and collected the blood in a can. We figured that the blood was rich in nutrients that might help us regain some of our strength. We were all weak from working the pump and manning the tiller around the clock for the past five days, but our stomachs were not quite strong enough to handle warm turtle blood. After much gagging, we dumped the can's contents overboard to a host of sharks which had gathered when we dumped the turtle guts.

The meat was another story, however. We sliced it into thin strips, which we then soaked in seawater and hung up on netting to dry in the hot tropical sun. We called it "turtle jerky," and it served us well. For days thereafter we feasted on sun-cured turtle jerky. We ate it plain, with honey, and with Salsa Iglesia, a Costa Rican version of spicy Worchestershire Sauce. I can still recall my surprise at how delicious it was with honey—but then, I love honey-cured ham, so why not?

The following day (number seven) the winds and seas subsided even more. It was time to start sailing for home, but first there was a major problem that had to be attended to. Our round-the-clock pumping efforts were exhausting us. The storm-split seams of our aged vessel's hull were leaking like a sieve. Something had to be done about the water that poured constantly into the bilges.

Once again it was Dave who ingeniously solved the problem.

Fishing To Survive

He gathered up a butter knife and a handful of stuffing from the same cushions that had supplied him with the vinyl to shape into washers for the pump. It was all he needed to caulk the leaking seams in the hull.

Fortunately, the sharks that had been attracted by the turtle butchering the day before had left the area. Porpoises swam around the boat, an indication that it was safe to go overboard to do the caulking. As we dove beneath the boat, Dave and I were amazed to see the width of the gaps in the planking; no wonder we could barely stay ahead of the water flow with our single hand pump. We stuffed and stuffed, and managed to stem at least two-thirds of the leaks. For the first time in a week, we felt reasonably seaworthy once again.

Once the caulking was completed, we raised our sails. For the first time since that afternoon when the devil wind hit, we regained control of our own destiny. Our boat was going where we wanted it to go, not where the storm dictated. We tacked into a light east-northeast breeze in four hour increments—four hours to the north-northeast, then four hours to the east-southeast. We estimated that we were about 300 to 350 miles southwest of our starting point, somewhere near the Isla del Coco. We were heading home!

Also on that happy seventh day, we stumbled upon yet another blessing. Under a forward hatch that had been inaccessible in the rough seas, we found a veritable gold mine—a 10-gallon jerry can of aged but potable water, a five-gallon can of kerosene, a steel bucket and a sack of dry rice.

This time, I was the innovator—I built a stove. By pouring a small amount of kerosene into the steel bucket and using a short length of cotton rope supported by a pair of vice grips as a wick, I created a makeshift stove. At last, I could cook a hot meal.

We had several lighters aboard for lighting my "stove" each day, and for the next six days I cooked up rice and fish in the coffee pot. Each day I seasoned it differently, one day with honey, one with salsa and so on.

For fish I could still catch dorado pretty much anytime I wanted, but now that we were sailing, I was able to troll a feather jig from the baitcasting rod. I caught football-size tunas. I think they were young bigeyes, and they made great fish-and-rice.

I used a minimal amount of our precious water supply to make the rice, but we still had to ration our drinking water tightly. If our calculations were correct, we figured we should hit the coast sometime around the twelfth to the fourteenth day.

Finally on the thirteenth day since our departure from Playas del Coco, we saw land. We had hit the coast of Costa Rica near the town of Tamarindo—about 30 miles from our starting point. Although we all were 10 to 15 pounds lighter, and weak from hunger, thirst, and exhaustion, we jumped for joy.

We dropped anchor just off the beach and rode ashore on the surfboards. We must have presented quite a sight, staggering out of the surf and up to a small tavern on the beach—and ordering beer and ice cream.

We had survived 13 days at sea and one of nature's most violent storms, and made it back alive. Teamwork, ingenuity and a modicum of luck had kept us in reasonably good shape throughout the ordeal.

Fishing To Survive

Only when we radioed our arrival from the little hotel down the beach, did we realize the full impact of what we had done. All hope of finding us alive had been given up several days earlier. Shortly after our disappearance, George Hommel, a family friend from the Florida Keys, had flown down to Panama to organize and coordinate the air search. The Air Force had spent $280,000 looking for us, before finally giving up after 10 days of intensive efforts.

The searchers incorrectly assumed that our drift would be more affected by the current than by the wind, so they concentrated their search over an area to the west and northwest of our departure point. We were nowhere near where they were looking, having been driven far to the southwest by the howling winds of El Viento Diablo.

Our friends back at camp had long since flown back to the states with all our personal effects to help our families plan our funerals. Everyone we knew considered us dead—lost at sea. One search plane had even spotted some floating wreckage far at sea, and assumed it to be all that remained of our sailboat.

Although the experience of fishing to survive was a new one to me, and expanded my definition of fishing, I still considered some of my angling efforts during the harrowing 13-day voyage to be recreational.

While we were tacking toward home, I trolled a dorado-belly strip bait from the big spinning rod. I was trying to catch a sailfish—just for the fun of it.

23

A Tarpon
To Drown For

by Capt. Lee Baker

Fishing guides make their living by consistently guiding their clients to trophy fish and enduring any number of tribulations in the process. My own reputation as a guide has earned me a loyal following over the 20 years I have been a professional light-tackle guide. Many have become good friends. I have enjoyed one such relationship for many years with world-class angler and fly-fishing record holder, Billy Pate.

While it's not my intention to drown at work, I will jump overboard for a client, especially Billy Pate, and I very nearly did drown doing that one fine June day in 1988 in the tarpon-rich Gulf of Mexico off Homosassa, Florida.

The day started out like most days with Billy. He was after the ultimate dream of most saltwater flyrod aficionados, a 200-pound tarpon on fly. He had already taken most of the billfish species on fly, a feat likely to stand unmatched for years. He also holds the I.G.F.A. World Record for tarpon caught on fly since 1982, when he whipped a 188-pound fish on a 16-pound tippet off Homosassa. Ever since that day in May, 1982, he has not only sought the 200-pound super-tarpon grail, but also tried to beat his own record.

Which brings us back to the day I nearly drowned. A 3-M video film crew was along, hoping for good footage of Billy fighting a record-class tarpon on fly. They knew that Billy always followed the big fish, so they followed Billy in their camera boat. This was the best time of year and the prime location for finding such record-size fish. Here, during the second half of May and into early June, tarpon come to spawn over the vast shallows that lie off of Homosassa. Each year the area comes alive with sophisticated flats boats filled with world-class anglers and guides, each seeking a place in angling history.

Early that morning we moved out into five feet of water over a broad expanse of light-colored bottom known as "Oklahoma," which lies several miles offshore. The bottom drops off imperceptibly as you move westward into the Gulf of Mexico at a rate of about one foot per mile. We timed our departure so that we would arrive at the fishing grounds when the sun was high enough for us to spot fish. A high incoming tide made conditions ideal.

At 10 o'clock I spotted a big "bust" a mile away. We headed toward the breaking fish. We could see that the school was working from the inside out to sea, so I moved on an intercept course, then followed the school for about 15 minutes.

When I finally poled Billy's 18-foot customized Sidewinder flats boat within range, we found ourselves in six feet of water. From his vantage point on the platform high above the outboard engine, Billy cast a purple pimpernel to one of the larger lead fish in the school of rolling tarpon. The fly was one I had tied myself and consisted of purple feathers with a little bit of African Guinea fowl tied on each side—I should have called it a "Baker Special."

He stripped the fly only once or twice, and a big silver tarpon rolled up and swallowed it. You could see from the size of the boil and the broad expanse of his silver back that it was a super-super big fish. I realized that it was one of the largest I've ever put any angler of mine on, and Billy hooked up solidly.

The whole thing was on video. The 3-M crew had moved their camera boat close to ours and captured the entire scene—from the sighting to the cast and finally, the hookup. None of us had an inkling of what the day held in store for us. All we knew was that Billy Pate had tied into one helluva big tarpon—maybe a record.

When the fish first jumped, the video crew shouted over to us: "That's the baby we were looking for." They had hoped to record a flyrod battle with a large fish and the immense size of this one exceeded their expectations.

The hooked fish stayed with his companions, and for a good 45 minutes we couldn't break him away from the school. We were running a high risk of having the thin line cut by the fins or tails of the other fish in the school. Finally, with some fancy boat maneu-

A Tarpon To Drown For   163

vering on my part, Billy managed to pull the mighty fish away from the school; the beginning of a long fight on the fragile 16-pound test tippet.

I followed the fish using our two electric trolling motors but by midday both batteries were dead. I could have dropped the big outboard to follow the fish, but out of courtesy to other anglers in the area, we used the quieter electrics. Even at idle, the big outboard would have spooked every tarpon in the area.

The big tarpon first ran toward shore, into about two feet of water at one point. We could see his great silver back rise completely out of the water as we maneuvered through a treacherous, rocky area. It always gets tense when a big fish runs into shallow water. He can easily circle and put a belly in the line, which in turn can wrap around a rock. It doesn't take much slack in the line for this to happen. If it does, the battle is all over in an instant.

To make matters worse, the wind picked up and increased steadily throughout the day. By late afternoon, the gulf was feathered with wind-whipped foam, and a two-foot chop rose in the shallow water. The tarpon doubled back on us several times, running right under the boat. Billy's adept rod-handling and some skillful boat maneuvering kept us out of trouble. Working into the wind, moving toward deeper water, the fish continued to move offshore, doing everything possible to outwit us. Billy kept the pressure on the fish every minute.

By the time the sun was low on the horizon, we had already traveled at least 30 miles in pursuit of the fish. As we continued to work ever westward, following 15 yards behind the apparently tireless tarpon, the setting sun in our eyes was blinding.

At eight that evening the fish surprised us by turning around and heading back east. That's when Billy figured it was do-or-die time. He started bearing down, tightening down harder and harder on the fish. He was gaining better control because we now had the advantage of working down-sea.

Billy inched the tiring tarpon closer to the boat as the fish ran first to the right, then to the left. Although our kill gaff had an eight-foot handle, I needed to be closer than that for an accurate, effective shot.

I laid the big gaff out, along with two short-handled lip-gaffs and my heavy gloves. As Billy worked the fish ever closer, I somehow knew that this enormous tarpon was going to snatch me off my feet and into the Gulf of Mexico the instant he felt the steel point of the eight-foot gaff. I just emptied my pockets—wallet, money clip and all, and stowed them with my wrist watch under the console.

Billy stood behind me so that I could reach out with the gaff from the closest point in the boat to the fish. His flyrod arched over my head as he pumped the fish closer, bearing down with all the pressure the light tippet could stand.

Finally, it looked right. I leaned out over the gunnel, stretched as far as I could reach, and sank the steel point of the gaff as hard as I could. It was like hitting a solid oak tree, but I remember thinking that it was a solid shot. My intention was to pull the huge silver fish back toward me and pin him against the side of the boat with one sweeping motion, but as I pulled he dove straight down. The eight-foot handle of the gaff went down over the gunnel and catapulted me off my feet and into the water.

The next 10 minutes are a confused blur, but I remember snatches of panicked thoughts. The first recollection was of being underwater—and hanging onto the gaff handle for dear life. Howard West later told me that the fish pulled me about 200 to 300 feet through the water. He said I looked like a water skier, but all I remember is that my head was under water, and I was holding my breath.

The first time I kicked my way up for air, I remember gulping a lungful, twisting my head back and screaming, "I got the fish. I still got the fish." I could see the boat a long distance away.

I also remember worrying about the gaff and wondering if it was stuck solidly in the fish. When I first stretched to strike the fish, my hands were at the very end of the eight-foot handle. Now I needed to choke up on the handle to reach the spot where the hook was stuck in the tarpon. It was important to me to know where in the tarpon's body the hook was buried.

While gulping air each time I frantically kicked myself to the surface, I worked my hands down the shaft. When I reached the end of the handle, I could feel the back of the fish, and I knew that I had a good bite. The steel hook was stuck firmly through the fish's back behind the gills and just about even with the dorsal.

Each time I would kick myself up for a breath, the fish would power back down, taking me with him. On one of my trips to the surface for a quick gulp of air I remember hearing Billy screaming for someone to help me.

They were all scrambling around, starting the engines up, and moving to help. Billy was still fast to the fish, having backed down on the drag to keep from breaking off—just in case I lost my hold on the flailing gaff handle.

After what seemed like an eternity, the sound man from the camera boat dove into the water as the cameraman in Billy's boat steered it alongside me and the tarpon. I could barely drag myself up into the boat, despite its low freeboard.

Once I climbed aboard, many hands joined mine on the handle of the gaff. It took four of us to haul the tarpon aboard—it was indeed a monstrous fish. Still sputtering and half-drowned, I tied it off securely, and congratulated Billy on his catch. He thanked me for the sterling gaffing job and my tenacious swim. We decided we were somewhere off New Port Richey, some 35 miles south of Homosassa. In the 10 hours since hookup we had covered considerable ground, indeed.

The trip back to Homosassa was slow going. Much of the two and a half hour boat ride was either in pitch darkness, or along rows of confusing shoreside and offshore navigation lights. We ran a few miles farther offshore to avoid a stretch of bad rocks and submerged bird racks, vestiges of a guano-gathering operation dating back to World War II. Barely visible in the daytime, they're almost impossible to see at night.

When we finally arrived back at the dock at Homosassa, the thoroughly bled and drained tarpon tipped the official scales at 184½ pounds, less than four pounds shy of Billy's existing world record. It was, and is still, the fourth largest tarpon ever taken on fly, and I'm proud to have played a role in its capture.

Had I drowned in the undertaking, however, I would have wished it would have weighed at least four more pounds.

═══ 24 ═══

The Unwelcome Guest

═══ by Don Slipka ═══

Whenever I'm fishing with friends on a charter boat, and someone hooks a mako shark, I make a beeline for the ladder to the flying bridge. I'm not chicken, mind you. I just remember a particular fishing trip about five years ago when I learned it is the best place to be when one of those devils realizes he's hooked. There's nothing worse than an angry shark.

I've been an avid sportfisherman for most of my adult life, and I especially enjoy big game fishing. I've fished in many places in the world, but one area is special to me.

The South Pacific, and especially Australia, has held a particular attraction ever since World War II. I was in the Navy in those days, stationed on the *Lexington*. I was wounded during the battle of the Coral Sea in 1942 and spent quite some time in St. Vincent's Hospital in Sydney, Australia. I really liked the Aussies and made a number of good friends there during my stay. Some have kept in touch to this day.

After my hospitalization, I returned to active duty until my discharge in 1946. Ever since that time, I have returned to the area frequently, and have fished all over the South Pacific. I have wet line regularly from Fiji to New Zealand, and all along Australia's Great Barrier Reef. I even bought the *Sea Venture*, a 46-foot Chris Craft in 1984 that two partners and I charter out of the marina at Cairns in northern Australia. The marlin fishing near Cairns is probably the best in the world, and although my home base is in Minnesota, I am able to sample it often.

Each year during the fall the marlin that frequent the waters near Cairns migrate down the coast of Australia, then travel around the southern waters of New Zealand and up the Pacific side to the area near the Bay of Islands. They arrive there around January, and remain for a while to feed—which is why the fishing around the northern tip of the northernmost island of New Zealand can often be incredible early in the year.

In 1985, on one of my frequent visits to the area, I found myself in the Duke of Marlborough Hotel with a bit of time on my hands. I contracted to charter Capt. Frank Griffith's 30-foot boat, the *Double Strike*, for a deep-sea fishing trip, and subsequently met a couple of personable chaps at the hotel who wanted to accompany me and share expenses.

Chris Hutchings was from Salisbury, Rhodesia, and worked for Coca-Cola. He wanted to go along just for the ride, and to take photos, which sounded great to me. He could shoot pictures of the trophy fish I *knew* I was going to catch. He insisted on paying his share, which was also fine.

John Plum was from Leeds, England—and he wanted to fish. Since the boat had two fighting chairs in the cockpit, it worked out perfectly, and it would only cost each of us $200 a day. It was a small price for what promised to be some major marlin action.

The following day dawned beautifully bright and sunny. The seas were calm when we pulled out of the marina at Pihia, and in short order we were casting for little, mackerel-like fish to fill the bait tanks mounted at the stern. The fish averaged about two pounds—the perfect size for enticing hungry marlin. John, our mate, deftly sewed 13/0 marlin hooks in the fresh baitfish, and by about 9 a.m. we were ready to pursue bigger game.

When we were about a half mile out from the harbor, where the water drops off to greater depths, John put out a colorfully-painted wooden teaser and Frank began letting out our lines. He was holding my line in his hand as he fed the bait back behind the boat, when suddenly, something nailed it. There was no toying around or indecision—the fish just grabbed the entire bait and ran with it.

Letting my line go in a flash, Frank hollered "mako" as I flipped the reel from freespool to strike drag and hauled the rod back hard. The hook was solidly set, but I wondered how John knew what was on the other end. It didn't jump as a marlin—or a mako—normally would.

John quickly answered my unspoken question. "I can tell by the way it hit," he yelled.

Mako sharks are one of only two species of sharks which characteristically leap clear of the water when hooked, the other being the smaller inshore species, the greater blacktip. Closely related to the great white, this member of the mackerel shark family is known to attain weights in excess of a half-ton.

Although found worldwide in tropical and temperate seas, these solitary, pelagic eating machines are found in the greatest numbers in the waters of Australia and New Zealand. In fact, most of the world-record makos caught on rod and reel have been taken from these waters.

An intensely active fish, the mako is the undisputed leader in attacks on boats. When hooked, it will unleash all its fury, reportedly leaping as high as 30 feet out of the water. It will frequently charge and bite a boat. In short, a mako shark is one tough customer—and I had a hefty one on the other end of my 50-pound test monofilament line.

Within 30 minutes, however, I had him to the boat. There was no doubt—it was a mako, a big mako. Chris took a couple of quick photos before the shark caught sight of the boat and took off. Line stripped from the Lor-Sol reel so fast that the side plates became too hot to touch, and the powerful fish didn't stop until he had stripped more than 200 yards of line from it.

Frank put the *Double Strike* into reverse, and great clouds of black exhaust smoke billowed back into the cockpit. Water poured over the covering board as we charged backwards after the fish. I blinked hard to clear the smoke and salty seawater that filled my eyes, and cranked furiously to regain line.

Once again, as soon as the giant fish got within 20 feet of the boat, he took off like a scalded cat. This time, he exited in great, greyhounding leaps. His immense body was clearing the water by 15 to 20 feet, and I remember wondering how he managed to summon the incredible strength to propel such bulk so far out of the water. When he finally quit jumping, he continued to strip off still more line—more even than on his first two screaming runs.

This time, it took me 30 minutes to regain all the line I'd lost and bring the fish into the boat. We figured the battle was over.

The fish must surely be exhausted from all that running and leaping during the last hour and a half.

We figured wrong.

Suddenly, from about 12 feet behind the boat he leaped twisting and turning high into the air—smack into the cockpit. All hell broke loose.

I unclipped my harness, leaped from the fighting chair, and charged toward the ladder to the flying bridge. John Plum was already ahead of me. The monster shark's flailing tail began splintering everything in the cockpit. As the mako slammed around the deck, his jaws snapped and bit at whatever his massive head smacked into. Bits of rods, gaffs and buckets went flying. Both bait boxes went overboard. Debris was scattered everywhere.

The mate tried to nail the moving target with a big gaff, but the creature smashed it to smithereens as if it was a toothpick. Frank was doing a mad dance around the deck, trying to slip a heavy tail rope around the tail of the still-lively beast. It whipped its tail at Frank, caught him at the knees, and swept him off his feet onto the deck.

The rest of us, meanwhile, were watching the awesome sight from the reasonably safe vantage point atop the flying bridge. Chris was too shaken to get many pictures of the madhouse below. The shark was virtually destroying the boat.

Suddenly, we saw Frank dash into the cabin, and emerge seconds later with a .30-06 rifle. He had decided, obviously, that the desperate situation called for desperate measures.

"Stand clear," he shouted to the mate—and proceeded to pump four high-velocity rounds into the mako's head. The thrashing creature slowed, and the two men were finally able to hogtie it with heavy ropes. They then hoisted the bloody beast out of the boat and lashed him securely to the stern platform while Chris, John Plum and I breathed a collective sigh of relief before descending to the now-safe cockpit.

We surveyed the damage. There was a hole in the side of the boat, smashed out from inside the cockpit. Fortunately, it was well above the waterline. A fortune in expensive fishing tackle lay splintered all over the place. It had been reduced to worthless rubble by the shark's assault.

After cleaning up the mess, Frank remembered a final detail. He lifted the hatch and proceeded to insert plugs into the holes in

The Unwelcome Guest

the boat's bottom made by the .30-06 bullets. The rounds had passed through the mako's head, through the decking, and on through the bottom of the fiberglass hull. He would make more permanent repairs back at the dock.

We decided to keep fishing. We had come for marlin, and we hadn't yet raised one. Frank pulled two undamaged rods from the cabin and rebaited. Once again, we began a trolling pattern.

Four long hours later, we spotted a black marlin feeding at the surface. Frank turned the boat to present our baits, and in short order John Plum hooked the respectable black. It put on a spectacular jumping exhibition—but out in the Pacific, not in the boat. It was a beautiful trophy and would look great on Plum's wall back in England.

Late in the afternoon, we arrived back at the dock in Pihia, where a crowd had gathered to see the double catch we had reported on the radio. We assumed that four .30-06 rounds, plus nearly five hours in the blazing sun, would have tolled the mako's death knell. But when Plum stepped over the "lifeless" body on the dock, it snapped its massive, snaggle-toothed jaws shut with a resounding "thunk," nearly taking his leg off. Plum came within an inch of getting nailed—the creature was still alive!

Carefully, *very* carefully, we hoisted first the mako, then the marlin on the scales. The nine-foot mako with his well-fed five foot girth, weighed an impressive 580 pounds. Plum's black marlin tipped the scales at 473 pounds. It had indeed been quite a day.

Later, as Plum, Chris and I were reliving the day's adventure back at the bar in the Marlborough, Frank brought the mako's jaw to me. I had asked him to cut it out, so that I could ship it home as a reminder of the experience. He had wrapped it in paper, then sealed it in a plastic bag, repeating the bagging process seven times—a bag in a bag, in a bag and so forth. I packed the whole thing in a large carton and mailed it home to Minnesota by express mail.

Four days later I called my sister from Sydney to tell her my trophy was on its way, and that I'd gone to considerable lengths to be certain that it was well sealed.

"It's already here," she screamed at me, "the post office called yesterday for me to get the stinking package out of there. "What do you want me to do with it?"

I told her to take it out and hang it high in a tree, far from the

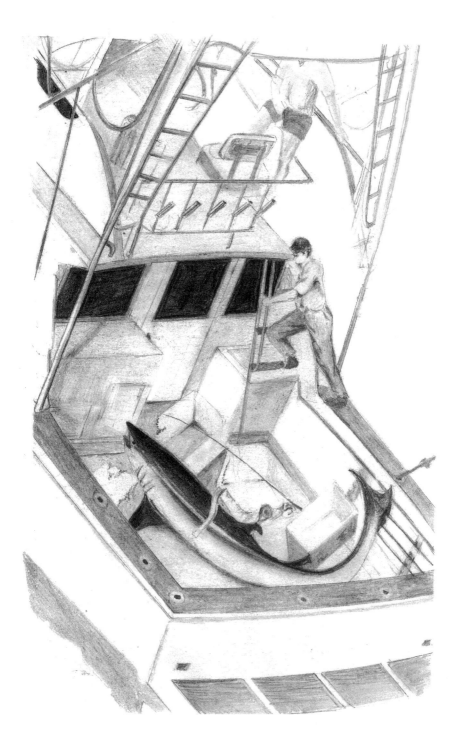

house. I explained that the Minnesota winter would keep it frozen until I returned home.

When I returned home two months later, sure enough, there was my mako jaw, ready to be cleaned and mounted as a permanent reminder of a marvelous and exciting day of fishing in the waters off New Zealand.

Now, as I gaze at the mounted jaws on my office wall, my thoughts drift back to the day I caught my largest mako. Although the jutting rows of long, sharp teeth are impressive, they don't begin to give a clue to the havoc a 580-pound mako shark can wreak in the cockpit of a fishing boat.

25

An Obsessive Angler

by Capt. Raphael "Chi Chi" Gonzalez

The people closest to me call me "Chi Chi." Like many Panamanians raised near the city of David in Chiriqui Province, I have always had a strong attachment to the sea. In this area, where so many people depend on fishing for their livelihood, we all take our fishing very seriously. But I also enjoy the sport of fishing. It has not only provided me with a fine living, it has given me much pleasure over the years.

In the course of my work as a guide, I fish with a great many anglers from all over the world, from first-timers to seasoned fishermen and women. I met many of these anglers at Club Pacifico on the island of Coiba in Panama where I worked for Bob Griffin. Most were carefree and noncompetitive about the sport and seldom got upset if they lost a fish.

Some, on the other hand, were downright obsessive in their intense desire to catch trophy fish. It was almost as if they had a powerful voice inside of them that measured their worth against their success in everything they did. Fishing to them was a win or lose proposition, and they felt crushed by defeat. For those fishermen, losing a fish was a personal calamity.

I'll never forget one such angler who fished with me at Club Pacifico. His wife fished too, but not with the same intensity. I'm not sure I ever really knew their names—I just called him "Doc" and his wife "Ma'am."

This wasn't their first trip. Doc had caught several black marlin at Hannibal Bank before, but this was the first time they had fished on my boat. I was happy to have them on board.

The day in question began like most March days at Club Pacifico. Parrots screeched overhead, as they flocked together in squadrons to head for the mainland to feed for the day. The sky was clear; not even a wisp of clouds could be seen. There wasn't a hint of a breeze. In a few short hours it would turn steamy-hot.

Doc, his wife and I headed southwest along the island shoreline in my little diesel-powered 23-foot Mako center console open fisherman. On our left, the lush green jungle spilled over the rocky shore all the way to Punta Hermosa. Swift currents twisted the slick surface of the sea like swirls of taffy. We left the island and continued southwest toward the open reaches of the Pacific.

An hour and a half after leaving camp, we arrived at Hannibal Bank and began fishing for live bait. Using a light spinning rod and a small yellow feather jig, Doc caught a fat little bonito. I rigged it with a bridle to a large 12/0 marlin hook and set it out to trail behind the boat on a heavy 80-pound outfit.

The rod was in the holder when suddenly the clicker began to scream. Doc grabbed the rod, flipped the lever on the big Penn Senator into gear and set the hook hard. For the next minute, a 300-pound-plus black marlin greyhounded away from the boat. Then, amazingly, the big fish turned and headed straight back toward us. Doc reeled frantically, trying to keep slack out of the line. Fortunately, the hook was set solidly and the fish didn't throw it.

No more than three minutes after the giant marlin ate the bait, Doc had him boatside. I thought of my boss's safety rule about not attempting to wire green fish, but only for an instant. All three of us were standing on the bow deck, Doc, his wife, who by now had a camera in her hands, and me. I had no choice—the leader was racing by me, well within my grasp.

As the fish ran alongside the boat, then past the bow, I grabbed the wire and held on with all my might. I expected the fish to try to jump away from the boat and the pressure I was exerting on the wire. Instead, the fish turned back toward the boat's port side, went under the craft, and came up on the starboard side.

Then, turning once again, it leaped from the water and *over* the bow of the boat, heading straight for us. By instinct, I let go of the leader and pushed the lady down all in a split second.

If I hadn't pushed her, the marlin's bill would surely have slammed into Doc's wife. She didn't escape entirely, however. After the 300-pound marlin cleared the starboard gunnel of the boat, the tail smacked her in the face. The fish's body completely cleared the starboard side of the boat, and only its tail bumped the port gunnel as it dropped back into the Pacific on that side.

Doc showed an incredible presence of mind. He dropped the rodtip when the fish first moved beneath the boat, and was holding the heavy rod high off the bow when the fish leaped over the boat. When the marlin bounced back into the water, the fishing line was clear of the hull.

As I moved to see if the lady was injured, Doc screamed, "I've still got him on!" He was facing the mighty fish, which by now was making great leaps away from the boat. He held on to the rod with a death grip, trying to work his way back along the side of the console to the fighting chair in the cockpit.

It was clear that the lady was seriously hurt. Blood spilled from her mouth and her nose was pretty bashed up. She didn't make a sound, but simply sat on the deck, holding her mouth. As her husband fought his fish, I wet a towel with ice water from the cooler chest and wiped the blood from her face. When she took her hands away from her mouth, I could see that several of her front teeth were gone.

"Is she all right?" Doc finally hollered from the cockpit.

"She got hit in the nose and mouth," I hollered back to him. Again he never even turned around. He simply told me to put some ice on her nose. All the lady did was lay on the deck and moan—Doc never said another word.

A half hour later Doc worked the now-tired marlin to the boat, where I smacked it with a hardwood billy club. The two of us managed to haul it over the gunnel and onto the deck. Only then did Doc look at his wife.

Now that his marlin was safely in the boat, he became the very model of a loving husband, comforting her and holding a piece of ice to her swollen face. "Let's head back to camp," he told me. I didn't need him to tell me; I was cranking up for home.

Back at camp Doc took a minute away from attending to his wife to check the scales. His trophy black marlin weighed 325 pounds. Afterwards, he promised to get his wife back to the states immediately. Cutting their trip short, they left camp the next day.

I still think of Doc and his wife now and then, but I hope I don't get any more clients like that. I like guiding dedicated anglers, but I find it much more enjoyable to fish with a client who values his wife—and friends—more than a trophy fish. Doc gave me a good tip, but I'll bet their dentist back home made the biggest profit from that fishing trip.

Complete Angler's Library

=26=

Skewered By
A Black Marlin

== by Colin Mizuguchi ==

Oahu, Hawaii, has always been my home. I'm a weekend fisherman and enjoy trolling for the wealth of offshore fish that populate these fertile Pacific waters.
Although I don't own a boat myself, many of my
friends do, and I fish with them almost every weekend throughout
the year. My favorite targets are skipjack tunas, yellowfin tunas
and dorados. In Hawaii we call them aku, ahi and mahi-mahi. I've
helped land aku up to 30 pounds, ahi as large as 100 pounds and
mahi-mahi up to 50 pounds, although these great food fish usually
average in the 20- to 30-pound range. Occasionally, I enjoy fishing for smaller reef fish close to shore, but my big love is still offshore trolling.

I've caught marlin, both blues and stripes, and I've helped
friends land these flying beauties. Most weighed between 50 and
150 pounds, but my biggest was nearly 200 pounds.

Last year, on Memorial Day, two long-time friends and I decided to run offshore to try our luck. The captain and owner of the
boat was Larry Park, a friend I had introduced to deep-sea fishing
only a couple of years earlier. Larry quickly became an avid fisherman and soon purchased a 16-foot Rynell tri-hull with a side console and a 70-horsepower Johnson outboard engine. Larry often
took off alone on weekends to troll for tunas and mahi-mahi, and
liked to take some of his catch to the auction block to help pay for
his gas when the fishing was good.

Ross Niyasato was the final member of our little group. A new father, Ross could only manage to get away to fish every now and then, and when he did, it was mostly for small inshore fish. He had never caught a big fish before. Although we planned to troll for anything that might bite, Larry and I were hoping to perhaps put Ross onto his first really big fish. Maybe even a marlin.

It looked like it was going to be a beautiful day. There were hardly any clouds, and the sea was mirror-smooth when we met at Waianae Boat Harbor at first light. We launched the boat and pulled away from the pier just as the sun crept over the horizon.

Although our boat was very small for big game fishing, we weren't really planning to venture far offshore. Our game plan was to head west about four miles or so, which would put us in about 300 feet of water. We knew that we shouldn't have to travel any farther than that to find tuna or billfish action.

The rods were set in the rodholders and our lures were laid out. We were using Shimano graphite rods and Penn International 80-pound class reels spooled with 80-pound test Ande Tournament line. Larry had skirted our assortment of lures himself. He was partial to red and black skirts with a little splash of orange on the black, although he also liked a green and yellow combination and an all-brown affair. Buying the heads and nine-inch skirts separately, he painstakingly glued the skirts to the heads.

Larry gave the word to put the lines in the water, and we dropped them back into position. Our lures bubbled and splashed behind the little tri-hull. Larry was at the helm and I was catching a catnap as we ran first to the west, then zig-zagged back toward the island, looking for fish.

Around 10 a.m., and two and a half miles from shore, the clicker on the right-side rod woke me up. Larry immediately punched the throttle for a couple of seconds to help set the hook.

As he throttled back, a black marlin took to the air and greyhounded away from the boat. We could see the little red and black lure trailing behind at the swivel clip as the energetic fish leaped repeatedly. It appeared that he was solidly hooked.

I leaped to clear the other lines and hollered to Ross to reel one in before taking the rod with the fish on it out of the rodholder. Larry kept one hand on the wheel while he reeled in the last rod (still in the holder) with his free hand. Then I grabbed all the rods and nearly threw them onto the forward deck to get them out of the way. The small cockpit had precious little room as it was.

Skewered By A Black Marlin

Then, and only then, did we strap a gimbal belt onto Ross, who by now was holding onto his rod for dear life as the marlin continued its jumping exhibition. We sat him on the cooler and clipped a makeshift harness (actually a fat rope with an eye-hook on each end) to the reel lugs.

We had found Ross his big fish, and were giving him all the encouragement we could. "Take your time," we shouted to him. Then: "Come on now."

We told him to pump back, then reel fast as he moved the rod forward. We continued to tell him what to do every step of the way and within 20 minutes, Ross's marlin was coming up about 30 feet behind the boat.

I put a heavy glove on my left hand and grabbed a gaff with my right as I watched the swivel clip break the surface, followed by several feet of the leader.

With my left hand I grabbed the leader and took a double wrap. I could see the fish several feet beneath the surface, its great eye staring right at me. I looked it in the eye, but it was too far away from the gunnel to reach with the gaff.

I remember noticing that the marlin's tail was sweeping hard from side to side. There was no doubt that this fish still had a great deal of life left in it, and that the heavy, 80-pound tackle had allowed Ross to pump it to the boat too quickly.

I let go of the leader and laid the gaff back down on the deck. "It's too green," I hollered to Larry. "We better drag it a little longer to tire it out more."

Seconds after I let go of the leader, the fish suddenly switched tactics and dove straight down. The tip of Ross's rod jerked downward from the sudden surge and smacked into the boat's railing.

"Don't let the rod hit the rail," Larry and I yelled in unison. We didn't want to break the rod. "Hold on—don't let go. Hold on—hold on!"

As we were still yelling, the rod, which had been bent into a deep bow by the sudden surge of the fish, straightened out and the line went slack. "He's unhooked," I thought to myself.

All of a sudden, I saw this great splash about 20 feet behind the boat. The still-green black marlin rose suddenly from below, leaped clear of the surface of the sea in a great geyser of water, and arched straight toward our little 16-foot boat.

I was standing at the stern, gaff in hand, when he flew into the cockpit, bill-first, like a missile. As he slammed into me, his bill punched a deep hole in my chest the size of my fist, then miraculously pulled back out again. His heavy body slammed down into the cockpit at my feet, his great tail beating a tattoo on the deck.

I remember I was still standing. The blow didn't knock me down, but the bill of the marlin had penetrated my chest near my left nipple.

It took me several seconds for the full impact of what had happened to really sink in. "I don't believe it," I said. "It poked me in the chest." I covered the gaping hole in my chest with my still-gloved left hand.

"The damn fish poked me in the chest," I repeated to Ross, and lifted my hand to show Ross and Larry where I had been poked.

It was hardly a poke. The 13-inch bill of a 72-pound black marlin had penetrated my chest all the way to the back of my ribs. Only a now-shattered rib had prevented the bill from sticking out my back and skewering me altogether. It had missed my heart by a scant centimeter, but had punctured and collapsed my left lung. Ross said later that the hole looked like hamburger.

Fearful that my very life was oozing away, I clamped my glove tightly to the hole in my chest, as I watched Larry put a judo hold on the flopping fish. I remember watching him bridge his body over the fish with his right hand holding tight to the bill and his left hand pressing on its body near the tail. "Get the bat!" he yelled to Ross.

Ross approached that fish like a man possessed. He hit it as hard as he could, grunting with exertion with each stroke of the heavy ball-bat. Meanwhile, although in deep shock, I was beginning to gather my senses. I remember saying "Hey, forget the fish. What about me? Get me back to shore."

While Ross was now in a frenzy over what the fish had done to his buddy, Larry tried to crank up the outboard engine. It wouldn't start. I must have been extra alert from all the adrenaline pumping through my body, because I suddenly noticed that the thrashing marlin had knocked the fuel line from the engine. As soon as Larry reconnected it, the motor hummed to life and we took off for shore. It was a full five minutes after the accident before we finally got going.

It was then that I felt a searing pain in my chest. I hadn't noticed pain before then, but now it hurt like crazy, and I became very short of breath. I reassured myself that if I were going to die, I would already be dead and my fear turned to anger. I started yelling. I was suddenly as mad at the marlin as Ross had been. Fear gave way to anxious resignation. Now I was hurting and breathing very hard and praying I would reach a doctor while I still had a breath left in me.

Larry drove the boat as if he had a load of eggs. He eased the throttle each time we hit the smallest of swells and juggled our speed to smooth the ride as much as possible. He also got on the CB. "We have an emergency. We're about two and a half miles from shore," he shouted into the mike. He got no response.

Thinking something might be wrong with the radio, he requested a radio check. Several boats, far offshore, answered, "loud and clear." I still don't know why no one on shore heard our frantic calls over the CB, but it was clear that we couldn't alert the medics to be there waiting for us.

A long 30 minutes later we hit the dock. Ross jumped onto the pier, the gimbal belt still around his waist, and raced for the pay phone. I remember his asking Larry for a quarter. I would have laughed, if it didn't hurt so much, when Larry shouted that you didn't need a quarter to dial 911.

I didn't think help would arrive as quickly as it did. I was happy to see that ambulance pull up within five short minutes. A medic raced down the pier, jumped into the boat and asked me to remove my hand from my chest. When he saw the hole, he knew we weren't fooling. He helped me to stand and hoisted me onto the pier. Another medic was waiting with a gurney, and together they wheeled me back to the ambulance. As they closed the door, the only thing I remember was seeing Larry standing there, ashen-faced and covered with marlin blood.

During the half-hour ride to the Queen's Medical Center they gave me an IV, took my blood pressure, and kept asking me the same question, "How old are you?" I realize now that they weren't dense—they just wanted to keep checking to see if I was still alert. They removed my sunglasses and the glove from my left hand. All through the ordeal, I had kept both glasses and glove on.

During the ride, the pain became more intense. Air was escaping from my lung and building up behind my pectoral muscles. My chest felt as though it was swelling. Air pressure was building up inside me and tearing tissue inside my chest. Then, every few min-

Skewered By A Black Marlin					185

utes the air would hiss out of the hole. That really hurt.

When we arrived at the hospital, a bunch of people surrounded me. They couldn't believe that I had been skewered by a marlin. Then, as if I didn't already have enough trouble, an orderly ripped open the packaging around an alcohol swab and some alcohol splashed into my eye. When I yelped, they thought I had been injured in the eye, too. They never did understand that it was alcohol that had stung my eye.

After cleansing and sewing up the wound, they inserted a chest tube to re-inflate the lung. To do that, they had to make an incision about four inches to the left of the wound, under my left arm. Then they inserted a tube through the incision to inflate the collapsed lung. I remember the doctor telling me "It's only going to hurt a little bit." He lied. It hurt like hell.

In the hospital room they hooked me up to a bunch of machines, put me on oxygen and shot me full of expensive antibiotics and some morphine for the pain. I can remember Larry and Ross being there, but not much else.

Between the time of the accident and my arrival at the hospital, more than one hour had elapsed, but now I was safely under a doctor's care. There was no question that I was going to make it. Nine days later they released me from the hospital. Two months later I returned to work with strict instructions not to do anything too strenuous. Lifting heavy objects was out, but gradually I regained my strength. Several months later I was as good as new.

Now and then I still lose sleep, replaying in my mind how that marlin came out at me and how close that bill came to my heart. I think to myself, "If I had moved a single inch to the left just before the marlin hit me, it would have gotten me smack in the ticker. My life's blood would have pumped out of me like a fire hose."

But, I know I can't think like that. People have asked me if I "got religion" from the experience, but I simply tell them that I thank God I survived. That's all.

Now, I feel I've got to go out again and catch another marlin.

27

Until The Sharks Arrived

by Steve Pennaz

O ur fishing trip was, plain and simply, one of those excursions that provide as much joy in the planning and anticipation as in the actual fishing. The fishing itself lived up to expectations—that is, until the sharks arrived. Then our trip became a hair-raising adventure.

Seven of us made the trip, which was billed as the first-ever NAFC Adventure Of A Lifetime to the Caribbean coast of Costa Rica. We planned to fish out of the Rio Colorado Lodge which boasts light-tackle action for snook and tarpon both in the swift-running waters of the river itself, and in the brackish water seaward of the rivermouth.

We all met at Miami's International Airport one April afternoon, then caught the Lacsa flight to San Jose, the capital of Costa Rica. After overnighting in the city, we boarded a small plane for the short flight to the lodge located on the Rio Colorado in the northeast corner of the country. Boats were waiting to run us upriver to the fishing lodge. Just getting there was a mini-adventure in itself, but at that point, none of us could anticipate what real adventures awaited us.

After quickly locating our rooms and unpacking, everyone was back on the dock ready to begin fishing. NAFC Charter Members Dick Stoesser and Moe Mendel immediately headed for the rivermouth and the surf beyond, while Mark LaBarbera and I went upriver to seek tarpon in calmer water.

We watched several other anglers hook, then lose tarpon, but our plugs produced nothing. Back at the camp at midday, we learned that two other members of our party, Don and Becky, had jumped one tarpon, but lost it. Dick and Moe had found a honey hole. They announced that they had hooked 11 tarpon, landed one, and lost two to sharks.

"Lost two to sharks?" The simple statement made by Moe in passing stuck in my mind only briefly. "Pass the salt," I said.

After lunch Mark and I headed toward the surf, followed by Dick and Moe. When we reached the rivermouth, our guide, Ceasar, stopped the boat and instructed us to cast toward the shore. I protested when Dick and Moe continued past us to the spot where they had hooked all the fish earlier.

For the next hour, Mark and I cast up and down the shoreline to no avail. Then, almost imperceptibly, something nudged my Rapala. I set the hook instantly but missed. With renewed interest, I continued to work the area. Four casts later something hit my plug again. I set the hook hard.

Instead of jumping, the fish took off on a powerful run—but not with the blistering speed I would expect of a tarpon. I glanced over at Ceasar and gave him a "What is it?" look.

"Jack crevalle," he guessed.

Eventually I worked the fish to the boat. Ceasar grabbed the heavy mono leader and lifted, his gaff poised and ready. Suddenly, he tensed up and yelled, "Big snook, big snook," just as the fish took off on its final run.

The snook was too spent to go far and was boatside again within minutes. Ceasar slipped the gaff beneath the gill plate and lifted.

Held at chin level, the snook extended well below our guide's knees. After a few quick photos, we sped back to camp to weigh the fish. I knew that the I.G.F.A. 16-pound test record for snook was 34 pounds, 8 ounces. The fish at my feet looked fat enough to beat that mark.

The spring scale at the dock, however, registered an even 30 pounds. Disappointed, I turned my near-record snook over to the camp chef to prepare for supper that evening. Then we insisted that Ceasar take us out to Dick and Moe's tarpon hotspot.

Dick was fast to a tarpon when we arrived, but he and Moe were having trouble. The rough surf was tossing their small aluminum johnboat, and the tarpon was swimming around and around

the boat. Dick was forced to constantly twist around to face his fish and at the same time struggle to maintain his footing on the water-slick deck of the pitching boat.

Then, just when Dick was beginning to gain the upper hand, the water exploded near the boat and a shark claimed his fish. I couldn't actually see the shark hit the tarpon, but when Dick hollered over to us to tell us what happened, a cold chill went down my spine. Mark and I both jumped fish before the day ended but they either broke off or spit the hook before we could boat them.

When I climbed onto the dock, I just happened to glance at the scales that several hours earlier had pronounced my snook less than record-setting weight. There was something peculiar about the needle—it was resting a full seven pounds under zero. That evening, we all ate my "world-record" snook. Everyone thought it delicious, but each time I took a bite, I could see my name in the record books.

The following day I paired up with Dick Stoesser and his guide, Orville, and we headed straight for the mouth of the river. The surf was up outside, and we had to very carefully thread our way through the huge breakers that extended completely around the rivermouth. Just beyond, however, we found a relatively calm patch of sea that was alive with a pod of anxious tarpon.

Within a half hour the first tarpon ripped into my Mirrolure and headed for the Nicaraguan border.

Fifty yards from the boat the tarpon took to the air in a tremendous leap and crashed back into the surf. Again the silver fish catapulted itself out of the Caribbean before taking off on another powerful run. There was nothing I could do but keep the rod high and hope my 16-pound test line would hold.

The fish was spent when I finally led it back to the boat about thirty minutes later. With Dick's encouragement, I pulled the fish toward Orville, who waited with gaff in hand.

Suddenly, the water blew up in our faces, and my line went slack as the tarpon disappeared in a huge, bloody boil.

"What happened?" I asked in amazement.

"Shark," said Orville as he calmly reached into his bag for a new leader.

"The same thing happened to us yesterday," Dick sighed. "Moe and I lost a number of fish to sharks. You won't believe how many are out here!"

Orville reached over the side of the boat and started splashing. "Wanna swim?" he asked with a sly grin.

Dick and I turned toward each other and laughed nervously. It wasn't really funny, especially when I recalled something I had heard some months before our trip. I had been trying to push the report out of my mind for days now, but it kept creeping back every time I heard the word "shark."

It seems that last year, at another rivermouth camp along this same coastline, a stateside angler had persuaded his young guide to motor through the crashing breakers beyond the mouth of the river in search of tarpon. This, despite the camp operator's decision that the high surf was unsafe that day, and that all boats were expressly forbidden to venture beyond the rivermouth itself.

As cooler heads feared, the surf was indeed too high for the small boat, and the over-eager angler's fragile craft capsized in the crashing surf. The angler was struck on the head by the flipping boat and drowned, while his young guide suffered a far worse fate. He was torn apart by the hungry sharks that populated the surf, despite the brave efforts of his peers, who tried to swim out to rescue him. The last they saw of him he was struggling frantically in front of a giant bull shark, that all could clearly see in a breaking wave scant inches behind him.

The scene flashed in my mind's eye, and I shuddered once again.

Dick had had enough. He wanted revenge. He had asked Orville to bring along a heavy, 80-pound class rod and reel and a strong steel leader, in case he got the urge to try to catch one of the beasts. After I lost my fish to the sharks, the urge came.

Minutes later, Dick caught a 10-pound jack crevalle. Orville immediately decapitated the fish with a long, rusty knife and let the carcass bleed into the water before impaling the head on a huge, steel hook.

Dick and I continued casting while Orville flung the offering into the heavy current and let it drift away from the boat. Then he tied a thick nylon rope to the rod and waited with his thumb on the spool.

The strike came about five minutes later. Orville suddenly hunched over the rod, carefully spooling the line out as a shark ran with the bait. I nudged Dick and nodded toward our guide.

Orville threw the big Penn into gear and set the hook as hard as he could, rocking our small johnboat in the process.

The stinging hook startled the shark into instant flight, surprising even Orville, who momentarily lost his footing and nearly fell in. He motioned for me to take the straining rod, but I passed the opportunity to Dick. "Go ahead," was his answer. "I'll spell you when he's a little less green."

Fighting huge, hungry sharks in heavy seas from a lightweight, 16-foot aluminum johnboat is crazy, but at the time we were so caught up in the excitement of the fight that we really didn't think about it. We simply rested the rod butt on the seat frame for leverage and cranked.

For the first half hour, the shark was unbelievably powerful. It would run hundreds of yards against the heavy drag, rest a bit while we worked it back to the boat, then do it all over again. Dick and I took turns on the fish. We had to. A constant downpour kept the bottom of the boat slick and slippery, preventing us from using our legs or back muscles during the fight. The lack of a fighting chair or even standup gear forced us to rely solely on our arms. They wearied quickly under the strain.

It was an agonizing hour before we were able to work the shark close to the boat. We finally caught our first glimpse of it as it cruised through the top half of a big swell. It was an enormous bull shark!

For the first time, doubt set in, and I again flashed back to the grisly scene that occurred months earlier at a similar rivermouth. It was the same kind of shark that had killed the young guide.

"Orville," I yelled over my back, "what are we going to do with this fish?"

"Just leave it to me," came his reply.

Strangely, that was all I needed to hear. I pumped a few more times, then turned the rod over to Dick.

The fish was close now. Orville waited with his gaff in one hand and a wooden club in the other.

When the shark was boatside, Orville moved quickly. He buried the gaff inside the corner of its open maw and brought the club down hard on the tip of the shark's nose. The hit wasn't solid, so he lifted again and brought the wood down a second time. Failing to kill the thrashing fish, he screamed at me to help deliver the coup de grace. I grabbed the club, bringing it down again and again. Blood flowed out of the shark's mouth into the water.

Until The Sharks Arrived

Orville had trouble hauling the huge shark into the boat so I grabbed a gill and helped heave. The mighty fish was soon resting at our feet.

Neither Dick nor I had ever seen such a fish, let alone landed one. We were so excited, the thought of other sharks beneath our little boat never entered our minds. Anxious to return to camp with our trophy, Orville started the motor and began to pull on the anchor rope.

Without warning, a tremendous wave broke over our over-loaded little craft, sending us on a wild ride down its face. We jerked to a sudden stop as the boat reached the end of the anchor rope. We were in grave danger. If we were lucky, the heavy seas wouldn't claim us. If we weren't lucky, the sharks would.

We could see the calm water of the rivermouth a scant 200 yards away, but huge waves were breaking between us and the safe haven. As Orville quickly lifted the anchor, restarted the motor and pointed the little johnboat toward home, Dick and I frantic-ally bailed with the only thing we could find—our shoes.

Orville kept our frail craft and its bulky cargo on the backside of a great, rolling swell, taking care not to let the wave behind overtake us, or allow our bow to get too far up on the crest of the one we were riding. We literally surfed to safety.

Once in the calm of the river, we breathed a collective sigh of relief, and held on as Orville raced full throttle for the lodge.

Fear forgotten, the thrill of victory returned, and the brief nightmare of our brush with death dissipated. At the dock, the shark measured $8^1/_2$ feet from tip to tail and weighed 257 pounds. Its mouth was wide enough to bite a 100-pound tarpon—or a man—in two.

As we hoisted the giant shark for photos, Dick and I decided that we had experienced about enough adventure for a while—well, at least until the next cold winter night in Minnesota, when it would again be time to begin planning another trip.

28

The Record That Almost Wasn't

by Don Mann

S tatic crackled on the VHF, then came a voice screaming, "It's a big, big fish! I mean a damn big fish! It may go 1000!" However, Larry Martin and his friends aboard the sportfisherman *Xiphias* didn't realize how big it really was. Neither did we, and we were trolling right behind Larry's boat.

For the crew of the sportfisherman *Xiphias*, the day had started as a lark, a busman's holiday out on the blue water. Normally, Larry Martin of Pompano Beach, Florida, worked as mate. But this day, Saturday, August 6, the boat's owner, Ralph Gilster, wasn't fishing and the *Xiphias'* captain, Barkeley Garnsey, decided to spend the day shopping in Charlotte Amalie on St. Thomas. Larry, another mate, Jimmy Unrath, and Garnsey's visiting brother-in-law, Jim Andrews, decided to spend the day fun-fishing at the dropoff north of St. Thomas. Unrath, who had never captained before, was given hasty instructions on how and where to run the boat as they set out from Black's Lagoon Fishing Center at 8 a.m. They intended to release any marlin they might catch.

George Cooper and I had departed from nearby Johnny Harms' marina just an hour earlier, aboard Mike Benitez' 53-footer, *Sea Born*. We were all heading north the same way, between Thatch and Grass Cays, past King Rock, between Tobago and Little Tobago Islands, then on northward about 12 miles to the dropoff. It is there that the prevailing easterly winds of summer push food west from the 35-fathom bank over the underwater cliff that drops to 100 fathoms plus. And it is there that blue marlin congregate in the summer months to feed on the countless schools of bonito, tuna and other feeding predators.

At 10:15 a.m. George Cooper tagged and released his first marlin. At 10:15 on the *Xiphias*, Jim Andrews had his first strike about a half mile in front of us. The hook pulled almost immediately. It was Larry Martin's turn minutes later, when the other rigger was hit. The knockdown was not followed by a hookup, but the same fish immediately went to the flatline. It promptly spit the hook.

The *Xiphias* had had three strikes in as many minutes, and missed all three. From the bridge, Unrath could see that the fish were in the 200- to 300-pound class.

Jim and Larry replaced the mauled baits on all the lines as the boat trolled on, circling the same area.

At about 10:30 a.m. they saw a fish moving straight up on the flatline, pushing a mound of water ahead of it like a submarine. Jim Andrews grabbed the rod and free-spooled when he felt the strike. The fish didn't eat the bait, however. About 10 seconds later, the fish reappeared, but not on the rig Jim was still holding. Instead, it crashed the mackerel on the right, long rigger.

Larry Martin grabbed the rod and set hard. The fish immediately began to smoke the 125-pound monofilament from the reel as Andrews hastily got the other lines in, and Unrath turned the *Xiphias* to chase the fish. When everything was in the boat, Jim Andrews quickly put on his wiring gloves, while Larry furiously cranked the big reel to put the slack back on the spool. Unrath turned the boat's stern toward the fish and backed down hard. Jim lay the fishing pliers on the chair, next to Larry.

All of this happened in a matter of minutes. All the while the fish was jumping, but no one was really watching. They were too busy cranking the reel, getting lines in, trying not to cut off the line while maneuvering.

Since the intention of the group was to simply enjoy a day of fishing and release any fish they might catch, the flying gaffs had been disassembled and stowed out of the way. All they really needed were the pliers on the chair beside Larry.

The fish hadn't been on for more than five minutes when Jim Unrath had backed down close enough to the fish for Jim Andrews to grab the 23-foot leader wire in his triple-gloved hands. Larry got ready to cut the wire for the release.

As Jim wrapped and then hauled about half the wire, the marlin was rising straight up toward him. It rolled slightly. Although the head didn't look particularly large, the sight of the massive bulk of that immense body rolling into full view was like nothing he had ever seen. It was this view that he later described to me as "a giant egg with a bill in front." He realized then that he just might be staring down a thousand-pounder.

He screamed, "Don't cut!" Larry had not yet cut the wire and was still in the chair. He slacked the drag as Jim let the wire go, and the fish took off once again, ripping off line with great, greyhounding leaps. Unrath backed down recklessly to keep the fish from stripping the reel. After 10 or 12 jumps, the fish settled down to a hard, steady run near the top, and Larry furiously regained line as Jim continued to back down hard.

Meanwhile, I had hooked a marlin, but it got tail-wrapped and pulled the hook when it started to go deep.

Just as I lost my fish, we heard Jim Unrath calling over the VHF, "We're going to need some help with this fish." And again, "It's a big, big fish. It's gotta go 1,000 at least."

I called up to Mike Benitez in the flying bridge, "Maybe we better get up there to help those guys."

"No need," said Mike, "the Striker is moving in to help."

We could see the Striker, the *Bruja Mar*, racing toward the *Xiphias*. Capt. Gary Richardson transferred mate Peter Gansz while Larry was still fighting the fish, a neat trick, bow to bow, in somewhat choppy seas. The fight continued, with the big fish jumping yet another dozen times.

Finally, Unrath maneuvered the boat into position where Gansz could grab the wire and Andrews could sink the first gaff. The two of them could barely hold the flying gaff rope as the fish churned at the end of its 20-foot length, thrashing the water white. After several minutes of this punishment, the two of them finally regained authority and hauled the giant fish close enough to sink a second gaff.

There was no more fight left in the big marlin. They had her this time. It was about 11:15 a.m.

But she wasn't in the boat yet. The combined efforts of all aboard could only manage to get the fish through the transom door as far as its gill plates. Their estimate that this had to be a 1000-pounder seemed certain as they fruitlessly tugged to try to boat the fish. They needed still more hands.

It was at just this point that they saw several sharks about 100 feet behind the boat. They knew that one bite disqualifies an IGFA record. No shark was going to mutilate their fish.

They quickly tied the head to the stern cleats and the bill to the fighting chair, leaving the bulk of the fish trailing behind the stern through the open transom door. Unrath gunned the *Xiphias* along at 10 knots to escape the sharks, and tersely radioed their problem, "Sharks!"

The *Bruja Mar* once more got into the act. Capt. Richardson gunned the big Striker into the *Xiphias'* wake, roared his big engines and steered in a zigzag pattern to drive off the sharks and buy Martin and company enough time to boat the marlin. At Unrath's request, Richardson transferred two more men to the *Xiphias*—his other mate, Jim Hardee, and angler Dev Moring.

Six husky men were then able to get the entire fish through the transom door, except for part of the tail. They lashed the door closed as far as it would go for the trip home.

From the comments on the radio, everyone in earshot began to realize that this fish would surely beat the 1,142-pound record set in North Carolina in 1974. Guesses of its weight filled the airwaves. Capt. Benitez called for dimensions. He had landed a black marlin off Australia in 1973 that had weighed 1,162 pounds. This blue was bigger.

Several boats were calculating as the crew of the *Xiphias* sang out the awesome statistics. The girth was estimated at 78 inches. (It later proved to be officially $76^1/_2$ inches.) She was fat right up to the tail. Hasty cockpit measurements put her length (notch of tail to lower jaw) at 12 feet, 1 inch. Later it was officially listed as 14 feet, 8 inches. The tail spread 5 feet from tip to tip.

Someone on the radio guessed 1,319 pounds, a surprisingly accurate calculation from some fancy figuring plus seat-of-pants factoring, based on the extraordinarily fat tail-third of the fish. Consensus seemed to settle between 1200 and 1400 pounds. It was truly the "Big Mama" that anglers had been seeking in these waters for many years.

Other boats moved in. The *Pescador* backed up to the *Xiphias* to transfer a bottle of champagne. They apologized that it was warm. Who cared?

We pulled alongside to take pictures, though all we could see was a giant mound of belly sticking up above gunnel level, and an enormous pectoral fin standing straight up from the center of the cockpit. The head was hidden from view somewhere up in the cabin, and the tail protruded from the transom door. There was much shouting from boat to boat, and congratulations echoed over the VHF.

The *Xiphias* called ashore for someone to try to find a scale big enough to handle the job, and certified to satisfy the IGFA. The call went out for Eddie Bertrand, the IGFA representative, to be on hand at the dock. Unrath headed the *Xiphias* home full bore.

At 3 o'clock the word flashed over the radio: 1,286 pounds, a new world record. The figure was later corrected slightly to 1,282 pounds when it was discovered that someone erred in weighing the board under the fish.

But it was the record, a solid, convincing record. The previous record was for a 1,142-pound blue taken by Jack Herrington off Nags Head, N.C. Martin's fish topped Herrington's by 140 pounds. Plus, it beat Elliot Fishman's Virgin Islands mark set a decade earlier by an amazing 437 pounds.

Back at the marina, hundreds of Virgin Islanders poured into the dockside area to view *their* record, returned once again. The excitement of several hours earlier aboard the *Xiphias* was still very much alive there on the shore. As I looked at the fish, it struck me that it was exactly a half ton heavier than my 282-pound blue taken the same morning. It was humbling.

Mingling with the crowd, later that afternoon, we watched as the big marina forklift tried to lift the fish onto a pickup truck. It hung over no matter what angle the operator tried. A flatbed truck would have been more appropriate to the task.

Several of the *Xiphia*'s crew were still milling around their prize. It would obviously take a long time for them to come down from such a high. As I talked to Jim Andrews about details that I hadn't picked up visually or on the radio, he was still shaky.

"You know," he said, "there were three bits of luck at work to-day. If we had hooked either of the other two fish that struck just before the big one, we would have missed the chance to hook her because we would have been fighting the smaller fish.

"And just as crucial," he went on, "was the split-second pause when I realized the size of the fish and caught Larry just in time, before he cut the leader wire.

His sun–split lips were visibly quivering as he spoke. "We came within seconds of releasing the blue marlin of all time."

29

Learning Young

by Frank Miller

C hris, my 12-year old son, and I had spent many pleasant summer days on Pawley's Creek, a small tidal stream that runs along the inside of Pawley's Island, South Carolina. There we caught blue-claw crabs along the shoreline, dove for clams in the muddy bottom of the shallow creek, and cast from shore for summer flounder. It was a perfect summer spot for a kid growing up.

This trip, however, was to be different. I brought along a 6-horsepower outboard motor in hopes of renting a boat to fish on the other side of the island (the ocean). I thought Chris was ready for more and bigger fish.

Rental boats were hard to come by at the island, but I finally located a 14-foot, v-hull owned by the local sheriff's son. He kindly delivered it to our dock in the creek.

We spent the remainder of the day in the protected waters of the familiar creek, checking out our motor and getting used to handling the boat. We even got in a little fishing. Tomorrow we would have to make it through the inlet's breakers. Even if the ocean were calm, the inlet would be a challenge.

That evening, we gathered our "ocean-fishing" tackle and respooled our freshwater reels with heavier, 14-pound test line, and replaced our No. 2 hooks with larger 2/0s. We were *ready*!

At dawn the next day we pulled away from the dock. Before heading for the inlet, we threw our castnet a few times into the tidal creek to collect some finger mullet for bait. The trip through the inlet's crashing breakers was scary, a brand-new experience for this pair of Kentucky bass fishermen. Fortunately, the ocean outside the inlet was calm.

Using small sinkers, we began drift-fishing, bouncing the live finger mullet along the bottom. I figured we might catch flounder, grouper, bluefish or, perhaps, sea trout.

What we did catch, however, were small sharks. Voracious little blue and hammerhead sharks attacked our live mullet baits with reckless abandon. Although they weighed from 3 to 15 pounds, they provided great sport on our light tackle. They were more fun than the little "lunch flounder" and blue-claw crabs we were used to catching back in the creek. We were having a ball.

As I released a blue shark, Chris suddenly got a solid hit, and set the hook equally hard.

"This is a big one," he cried.

"Well, set the hook again," I answered.

He repeated, "Dad, this is a *really* big one." His Mitchell 300 reel was spilling line at a great rate, and I suddenly wished that Chris had been fishing with my rod. His was missing six or seven inches from its tip after he had broken it off years before. It was bent nearly double by the creature Chris had hooked. Whatever it was, it was heading out to sea.

"I'm running out of line," Chris shouted back to me from his perch on the bow of the 14-foot boat.

I headed the boat in the direction of the running fish. Moving slowly, we kept steady pressure on the fish. Just as we caught up, and the line was straight up and down, the unseen fish ran off again with undiminished power.

Again and again, I would run the boat slowly toward the fish as it headed farther and farther offshore, and every time we got close, it would take off again. If this was another shark, why hadn't it bitten through the leader?

We caught up to the fish again. This time it lay on the bottom like dead weight, and wouldn't budge. Chris's arms were tiring, so I told him to switch hands, but to keep the pressure of the bent rod on the fish. I reassured him that sooner or later the fish would tire, and the fight would get easier.

As Chris held his rod high against his stubborn, unseen adversary, I thought of our gas supply for the first time. I hadn't refilled the tank, and we were already much farther out than I ever planned on going. Neither Chris nor I ever considered cutting the line. I told Chris that I would shut the motor off and only start up again when the fish began to move. Our gas was low, indeed.

Finally, the fish began to move out again. This time, I waited for Chris's signal that the line was low on the spool. Then, I cranked up and we repeated the process of regaining line as I motored slowly toward the fish. This time, however, Chris continued to gain line. Little by little he raised the fish straight up from the bottom. A brown shape appeared out of the murky depths, getting

bigger and bigger as it rose into view beneath the surface.

"It's a hammerhead," Chris shouted. And a hammerhead it was—a good 7- or 8-foot long hammerhead. No wonder we had had such a struggle with the fish. It was enormous!

"Now what?" I asked myself. We had no gaff aboard. We had no rope noose to slip over his head or tail, either. I did have a .22 pistol with me, however, and I decided that our best chance would be to maneuver directly alongside the fish for a perfectly-placed shot in its ugly, hammer-shaped head.

The shark was at the surface, so I eased the boat slowly toward him. Once again, he turned and made a short run around and behind the boat. He was facing us now, with the line running directly from Chris's rod to his mouth. He looked as though he was staring us down.

Several times I got him just about lined up for a perfect shot, but each time, he eased away, always on the surface, and always facing the boat. There was no doubt in my mind that that monstrous fish was plenty tired by then. He even listed to one side as he slowly waved his broad tail from side to side.

"He's whipped," I assured Chris, who was gamely holding his rodtip high to maintain pressure on his trophy. Just as I spoke, the great fish slowly twisted his body, gave one more flip of his tail and, as he turned, the slim, 14-pound test line brushed against his sandpaper hide and parted. Chris's rod suddenly snapped up straight, as the fish slowly sank from sight.

With aching arms and tears streaming down his face, Chris looked at me and said nothing.

"Chris, you won the fight," I said, with pride in my voice, "and he's alive to fight again."

"Maybe next year, when both of us are bigger, I'll meet him again," Chris replied as he stared into the empty depths.

30

The Ordeal Of Cool Hound Luke

by Don Hawksley

Before us, as far as the eye could see, stretched a solid wall of purple-black clouds. The top of the dark mass churned and folded like taffy in a mixer, and beneath it, separated by a sharp line of demarcation, a narrow layer of bright, light-grey clouds rested on the horizon. It was a frightening sight.

We were running hard to the west, heading back to the Conch House Marina in St. Augustine, Florida, after a successful day of offshore fishing. All day the seas had been as predicted, "three feet or less," and our happy crew of four men and a dog were elated over our success. Our fish box was full of hefty dorado and tuna, and a king-size wahoo that wouldn't fit in the box lay on the deck under a blanket of wet towels.

But the sight that suddenly appeared before us as we raced toward home was heart-stopping. A solid storm front stretched from south to north like an ominous curtain between our little boat and safe harbor, some 24 miles away. There was no way around it, and the nearest landfall back in the direction from which we'd come was Portugal.

Our 20-foot, outboard-powered, Mako center console skiff suddenly felt very small, and the nervous expression on every face aboard said more than words. We were in for it, and a feeling of impending disaster cast a pall of silent panic over our little group.

Frustrated by the inevitability of what lay before us, we nonetheless summoned enough presence of mind to make whatever simple preparations were possible.

We each put on a life preserver. There was none for the dog, but my 10-year-old companion, Cool Hound Luke, was a yellow Labrador retriever, a dog born to the water. He could probably swim better than any one of us, should the need arise.

One of our number, Bob Carpenter, was a licensed captain, so I turned over the helm to him. He maintained our course, directly into the storm and toward our destination, the marina.

Then, hearts pounding, we watched it come.

It had been an interesting weekend. I had picked up my brand new Mako that week, and planned to break her in at the Mako Owners' Tournament at St. Augustine. I didn't have time to make the little personal adjustments to the boat that I normally would have. When the weekend was over, I planned to re-mount the batteries in a spot above deck level, seal some of the openings to the inner liner, and add some other equipment. Although I had made certain that we had all the basic safety equipment aboard, I hadn't had time to install a Loran-C or backup bilge pumps. Still, considering that this was a maiden voyage, we were quite well equipped.

Although we missed the first day of the Mako Tournament, we managed to fish the second day, Saturday, with moderate success. The four of us agreed to stay over an extra day and fish Sunday to stock our larders.

Blessed with flat calm seas and a beautiful, sunny day, we set out at 7 a.m. Sunday for the long haul to the fishing grounds. From St. Augustine the continental shelf stretches for many miles, and you don't reach deep water until you've traveled east about 50 miles from shore.

We ran 45 miles in only an hour and a half—I was really pleased with the performance of my new rig. The 150-horsepower Johnson moved the fully-loaded 20-footer at a great rate, especially in such calm seas. When we came across the first weed line 45 miles out, it quickly became apparent that we didn't have to run any farther. The sargassum was populated by all manner of baitfish and trophy-size gamefish. It proved to be a bonanza.

Over the next several hours we landed a cooler-full of dorado averaging 12 to 15 pounds—one went a good 30 pounds. A 28-pound blackfin tuna soon joined the dorado in the box, and finally, a wahoo struck one of our trolled ballyhoo baits and tore

Complete Angler's Library

The Ordeal Of Cool Hound Luke

off line in a screaming first run. When we finally gaffed him and swung him aboard, he measured a full six feet and weighed in the neighborhood of 60 pounds—a real trophy. He was too long to fit in the already-stuffed cooler, so we laid him on the deck and covered him with wet towels to keep those great-tasting steaks cool and fresh.

Around three in the afternoon, as planned, we called it quits. We had enough fillets for all four of our freezers, and it was a long way home. It was the perfect capper to a great weekend.

But the weekend wasn't over, as we soon discovered. Halfway home we collided with the storm front as it moved due east—directly in our path.

At 4 p.m., 24 miles from shore, the storm hit us with all its fury. A great wall of water slammed into us like giant surf rolling over a hapless swimmer. Mountainous waves, driven by 70-mile-an-hour winds, crashed over our little skiff, and the temperature dropped precipitously. Bob tried to keep our bow headed into the 14- to 16-foot seas, while we hung on for dear life and tried to shield our faces from the stinging, gale-driven rain.

As the leading edge of the storm hit us, Bob managed to get off several Maydays over the VHF radio, and heard at least one acknowledgement from the Coast Guard on the other end. He was screaming into the microphone, trying to make himself heard over the din of screaming wind and crashing water. Each time he released the button to listen for a reply, the radio crackled with static and jumbled voices. The airwaves were cluttered with other Maydays from other vessels obviously in the same predicament as we were. It was clear that quite a number of boats had been caught offshore by this sudden, violent storm, and we wondered if the acknowledgement we heard was a response to our call, or to someone else's.

We were taking on water far faster than any bilge pump could possibly handle. Our two batteries were mounted in the hold, and the rising seawater quickly shorted them out. Our radio went dead. Then the outboard engine drowned as giant waves, striking us both fore and aft, completely swamped the boat. We were at the storm's mercy. Clinging to any handhold we could grasp, we crouched low as waves crashed over our heads.

Completely awash, the 20-foot Mako wallowed deep at the stern, her outboard engine completely submerged. The bow stuck up, looking for all the world like the Titanic in those last seconds before she slipped beneath the surface.

I hollered to my companions to help me lighten the boat. We threw the wahoo overboard, and a chair, then emptied the cooler of our remaining bait and all the rest of the fish—except one. I had the presence of mind to save one dorado (for cut bait) and the rods and reels, in case we had to fish for food later on. We chucked the tackle boxes and all the tackle except for a few jigs, which we saved for the same reason. And we tossed the seat backs. It wasn't much, but I figured that even a few pounds might help keep the hull riding higher in the water.

We kept the batteries, and the coolers, which held a few cans of soda and beer and several soggy sandwiches. I had forgotten to load gallon jugs of drinking water aboard, something I normally would not have left behind.

With the load lightened as much as I dared, the forward deck was only awash in about a half foot of water, and the water amidship (by the console) was only about a foot deep. We moved ourselves and the remaining gear toward the bow, and huddled low. Cool Hound Luke climbed up on the seat in front of the console, apparently unfazed by the chaos that raged about him.

It was at this time that we jury-rigged a makeshift sea anchor from a large bait bucket, and tied it off from the bow cleat. Despite the fact that it was not a real sea anchor, it nonetheless effectively kept our bow pointed into the wind. Since we were down at our stern, the raised bow helped shield us from the biting blasts of wind and at least some of the wind-blown water.

We all had to keep low while rigging the makeshift sea anchor and tossing gear overboard, because the force of the wind would have blown us overboard if it caught us standing upright.

For several hours giant walls of water continued to break over the entire boat, and the wind continued howling. By sundown, the wind had let up a bit and the seas subsided to about six-to-eight feet. Although breakers continued to wash over us, and the boat was lying low in the water, we felt reasonably secure huddled on the deck forward of the console. We were already as full of water as we could possibly be, so there was no fear of sinking. I remember thinking, as daylight turned to darkness, how fortunate we were that modern sportfishing boats are all required to be built with positive flotation. A few short decades earlier, if you swamped, you sank. I shuddered at the mental image of floating free in such a sea, held up only by a life jacket, a tiny speck alone in the open ocean. We were miserable, but we were still in our boat—and it was afloat, albeit a bit low in the water, to say the least.

If we had had any inkling of what the day held in store for us when we left home that morning, we would not have dressed as we did. Shorts and tee shirts are perfectly comfortable garb for a day's fishing on a balmy day in May under normal circumstances. These, however, were not normal circumstances. As darkness crept over us, the temperature dropped sharply. We were already soaking wet and chilled by the cold, driving winds of the storm, and the cold of night only compounded our woes. We were beginning to feel the effects of exposure, and each of us shivered throughout the night. I shook so hard my muscles ached.

It soon became clear that the water at our feet was considerably warmer than the air, so we huddled still lower and moved closer to the front of the console, where the foot-deep water provided a modicum of welcome warmth. There was no respite, however, from the waves of seasickness that swept over all of us from time to time, adding to our discomfort.

It was a long, cold, miserable, sleepless night—one I shall not soon forget. The constant noise of wind and waves was interrupted occasionally by the whap-whap sound of choppers overhead. Although we didn't know it at the time, the Coast Guard had enlisted the help of Navy helicopters to search for the countless boats caught in the storm. Near, yet far, they were searching for us.

In the middle of the night, we were first frightened, then comforted by new companions. All around the boat we could hear a strange sound of whooshing air. It was a school of porpoises. We finally figured that what we were hearing was the unmistakable rush of air being expelled through their blowholes. Although we couldn't actually see them, their presence made us feel more comfortable—we were not alone. And besides, we all knew that sharks were unlikely to venture into the middle of a school of porpoises.

Some time after midnight, we sensed that the winds and seas were subsiding more rapidly, so we tried to start up our kicker, a little 15-Hp Johnson mounted on the transom next to the big engine. Despite its thorough drenching, it actually started, although

it barely moved us. The load of a 20-foot boat, completely awash, was a bit too much for such a tiny engine. The little engine labored for awhile, then drowned in a wave, and quit for good.

Shortly before dawn, as the seas dropped still lower, we tried to drop anchor. Our 100-foot anchor line allowed the anchor to barely touch bottom, but we needed more scope for it to dig in and hold. I scrounged around in the forward locker and came up with a 75-foot ski rope, which I tied to the 100-foot anchor line. The additional length provided enough drag for the anchor to hold bottom. Although still swamped, at least we were no longer drifting in the current toward God-knows-where.

By dawn, the seas had dropped to a flat calm, and the warming sun was a welcome sight. As we dried off a bit, we could see fish breaking all around the boat. Several ships loomed on the horizon, but evidently our half-submerged boat was too far away for them to see. The sun rose higher, and at mid-morning we spotted a scuba dive-boat heading offshore. Firing our last remaining flare, we drew their attention and they turned toward us.

As they pulled alongside our half-sunken craft, they asked if we were all right and then radioed our position to the Coast Guard. They told us we were 18 miles from shore. We had drifted some six miles closer to land during the night. Amazingly, within minutes a chopper appeared overhead, circled, then dropped a sand-bagged streamer with a note smack into our laps.

The note listed signals by which we could communicate our situation to them, as they hovered overhead. By making various arm motions and waving particular items of gear, we were able to indicate to them that none of us were injured, that we still had some drinking water, and so forth. Within a half hour a Coast Guard cutter pulled alongside, and the chopper moved off.

They left us in the boat, rather then trying to transfer us at sea, and passed over a towline. Then they towed us hard, in order to drain most of the water over our transom and out of our boat. By the time we reached the dock, we were once more afloat, although we still had a considerable amount of water in our bilge.

The Coasties told us that the storm had been one of the most intense to hit that section of the coast in many years. Over 40 boats had been swamped between Jacksonville and Daytona Beach, but most of the people had been rescued late the day before. One man, however, had drowned.

It had been a frightening ordeal, but at last it was over. I never thought the simple act of stepping from my boat onto solid land could feel so good.

Cool Hound Luke evidently felt even greater relief. He leaped from the boat, bounded to the nearest patch of grass, and relieved himself. Talk about a housebroken, boat-broken dog! He had been holding it for 35 hours—ever since we left the dock the previous morning. Is that a super dog—or what?

31

The "Catch" Of A Lifetime

by Don Mann

There's one offshore gamefish most anglers know how to catch with regularity; it's the dorado or mahi-mahi. Resplendent in hues of gold and blue and green, this flashy speedster not only provides exciting sport on light tackle, it also provides mighty tasty fillets at the table.

Perhaps the greatest attraction of the dorado is its dependability. It readily attacks a wide variety of baits and lures, and is widely distributed over all the temperate and tropical oceans of the world. Locating great schools of these fish is relatively easy. All the angler has to do is head offshore and keep a watchful eye for either a congregation of feeding seabirds or floating debris. Beneath the birds and flotsam he's very likely to find dorado.

In mid-May, when the Florida Outdoor Writers Association held a mini-tournament as part of their annual conference at the Cheeca Lodge in Islamorada on the Florida Keys, our primary target was dorado.

I was assigned to fish on the magnificent 55-foot *Ultima Thule*, with Capts. Dietmar Kossman and Craig Murphy. We weren't at sea for 30 minutes when we found a large school of small fish close to the reefs. We caught a few, then moved farther offshore in search of larger fish. Every hour or so we would come upon schools of small- to medium-size fish. We would pause, catch a few, then continue our trek farther and farther offshore, still looking for pods of larger fish. We passed the south-bound shipping lanes, then the north-bound lanes, as we trolled ever southward. We were looking for floating lumber—and that one giant dorado that would win the tournament.

By 1 p.m. we were 21 miles from our dock at Bud 'n' Mary's Marina on Upper Matecumbe Key, when Dietmar shouted down from the bridge that he saw a giant log in the distance, with what appeared to be two seabirds perched on it. We turned to check it out. It was bound to be sheltering dorado, and maybe our trophy fish was among them.

As we drew closer, Dietmar called down to the cockpit, "My God, it's two Cubans on a small raft." We all strained to see the raft as it rose into—then out of view—in the heavy swells of the Gulf Stream.

The raft consisted of three large truck inner tubes, swathed in burlap, and tied together with yards and yards of heavy hemp twine. The tubes were mounted on heavy planking, and we could see several obviously empty plastic water jugs flopping on strings attached to the raft. A husky-looking man wearing what appeared to be a green uniform sat cross-legged in the front tube with a small paddle of bleached-white wood on his lap. He was waving his arms above his head. Behind him in the second inner tube, was a slimmer man who appeared to be in considerably more distress. He had trouble remaining upright, and periodically slumped over. Both men sat within the inner tubes, their legs crossed before them. In the third inner tube we could make out a couple of haversacks, a jacket and the plastic jugs.

As we trolled close by the raft for the first time, a large dorado consumed my ballyhoo bait and rose majestically into the air alongside the two men in the raft. I set the hook and jammed the rod back in the rodholder.

The men were waving their hands in the air and shouting "¿Estados Unidos?" It sounded more like a question than a declaration of salvation. Obviously, they had no idea where they were and wanted to be sure that we were, in fact, who they hoped we were.

We shouted back "¡Si! ¡Estados Unidos—bienvenidos a libertad!" Yes—United States—welcome to freedom! They smiled for the first time, weakly, and shouted back, "¡Gracias a dios!"—then pleadingly, "¿Agua?" Thank God, then, water.

Meanwhile, Dietmar was already on the VHF radio trying to contact the Coast Guard. They radioed back instructions to give the men water—and then *stand off* and await their arrival. They would pick the men up themselves. We were *not* to take them aboard.

I helped Craig toss a half-filled gallon jug of water to the raft. We could see that the Cubans' hands were swollen and wrinkled like large, white prunes. Although Craig made a perfect toss, the two men were unable to grasp the jug and it fell into the water. As the strong current carried it out of their reach, both men paddled frantically after it. One used the short wooden paddle, while the other used his hands. It looked as if one of the men was about to jump overboard after the jug, which by now had floated several feet out of reach.

I screamed, "¡No, no — otra agua!" We have more. Dietmar backed the *Ultima Thule* closer and this time they grabbed the second jug. One man was now slumped over in the raft, obviously exhausted by his paddling efforts. His companion passed the jug

back to him to drink first. It was a heart-wrenching scene.

When a fishing line brushed across my face as I stood at the transom, I suddenly remembered the dorado we had hooked earlier. I snatched the rod from the rodholder and, while we were "standing off" awaiting the arrival of the Coast Guard, landed the 24-pound dorado. The water around the raft was alive with very large dorado. The definition of "flotsam," floating debris that attracts open-water gamefish, took on new meaning, but thoughts of catching fish were wiped from all our minds by the sight before us.

After several minutes of watching the two men finish off the jug of water, I could stand it no more. I called up to Dietmar in the bridge, "How long is it going to take those guys to get here?" I knew that we were pretty far out to sea.

He replied, "An hour and a half. We're 21 miles off."

"Why don't we just *tell* the Coasties that we're taking the men aboard and will head straight for Alligator Light? Ask them if they can intercept us on our way in," I said.

Dietmar said tersely, "Take them aboard," and got back on the VHF to advise the Coast Guard of what we were doing. He backed the *Ultima Thule* down, as Craig opened the tuna door. I handed Craig a long-handled gaff to reach out and pull the raft toward our stern, and seconds later, the two soggy and exhausted men collapsed on the deck.

We wrapped heavy towels around their shoulders and gave them fruit juice, chicken and apples. Their bodies were shivering and they were obviously close to shock. They had barely enough strength to raise the food to their mouths. The husky one had cuts and abrasions on his arms and legs, and a nasty, raw wound on one foot. He had one boot on, but his companion was barefoot. Their hands and feet were horribly wrinkled.

Nonetheless, they had enough energy to repeat over and over again, "¡Gracias!" and "¡Libertad!" and glancing at each other, "¡Estados Unidos!" Thank you—freedom—the United States.

The Coast Guard got on the radio, once again. They instructed us to "take aboard all personal effects," and to "sink the raft," explaining that they didn't want the empty raft to be found later" and generate rumors of more Cubans lost at sea." At the moment, it made sense.

I leaned over the transom and gathered up the haversacks and

the jacket, and one boot that didn't match the boot worn by the husky man. The several plastic water jugs were empty.

We all wondered aloud how in the world the Coasties expected us to sink this raft—its base was made of wooden planks. I did all I could, slashing each inner tube with a fish knife, and turning the still-floating remains loose. It drifted off with its horde of dorado still hovering beneath it as we headed full throttle for Alligator Light and our rendezvous with the Coast Guard.

We managed to get the refugees' wet shirts off and bundled them in blankets. We learned that the huskier man's name was Victor Rodriguez Torriente. The other was Joaquin Guillermo Gonzalez Cotto. Victor was 23 years old. Joaquin was 22. They wandered off and slept on the deck during the ride in, their bodies wracked by occasional involuntary tremors from their incredible ordeal at sea. At that point, I had no idea of *all* the tribulations they had endured both before and during their incredible voyage.

While they slept, I noticed that Victor had tied a wooden-handled can opener and a tablespoon to his belt loop with a piece of twine. It wouldn't have helped to have canned goods aboard, and then lose the opener. On his wrist he wore a diver's compass on a rubber wrist-band. I could see that the bezel was set on 30 degrees, north by northeast. I wondered what use such a navigational aid could possibly serve, when they were strictly at the mercy of the powerful Gulf Stream. The small paddle would have been of little use, once the raft was being swept along by such inexorable currents.

As they slept, I examined the haversacks. One was empty, but the other contained two forks and five cans of food swimming in a mush of seawater, sargassum seaweed and soggy labels. I managed to carefully smooth one of the labels flat enough to read it. It was in Russian and pictured what looked like meat balls and pasta in tomato sauce. We surmised that most of the groceries on Castro's island must be imported from Russia these days.

We arrived near Alligator Light ahead of the Coast Guard boat, which had missed intercepting our course farther offshore. While we awaited their arrival, we helped Victor and Joaquin to their feet to see the distant shoreline—and their very first view of the United States. Victor's injured leg and foot wouldn't support him. It hadn't been weakness alone that caused him to collapse on the deck when he first came aboard.

As they both grinned at the sight, Joaquin said in Spanish to his older companion, "Thank you for saving my life." Only later was I to fully understand exactly what he meant.

When the Coast Guard boat finally pulled up, they put out fenders and put off two guardsmen onto the *Ultima Thule* to help transfer the refugees. Except for one hard crunch of gel coat when the two boats rose and fell into each other in an ocean swell, the transfer went without incident. I passed the men's shirts, jackets and haversacks over to the guardsmen, we waved goodbyes and then headed back to Bud 'n' Mary's.

The Coast Guard steamed off to the east and the Islamorada station with their charges. The two men were headed for medical attention at Mariner's Hospital in Key Largo, and thence to the Immigration and Naturalization Service (INS) detention facility on Krome Avenue in Miami for debriefing and processing.

We were convinced that had we not spotted the pair, their

course and distance from shore would likely have precluded rescue, and they would undoubtedly have died. Only later was I to discover just how desperate their situation really was when we happened upon them 21 miles off Islamorada.

During the following week I wondered how the two men were doing. Did they have relatives in Miami who would sign for them and take them in? How were Victor's wounds? And I wondered, too, about the rest of their story: How did they escape? How long had they been at sea? What powerful force could possibly motivate two young men to take such incredible risks? I wondered if they really understood the enormous odds *against* surviving such a journey.

Finally, one week later I called the district director of the INS in Miami and asked if I could visit Victor at Krome to interview him. He approved, and referred me to the detention center commander, Vinnie Intenzo. Intenzo approved as well, and we set up an appointment for the following day.

Since Victor spoke no English, I enlisted a close friend, Rick Alvarez, to serve as my interpreter. Rick was born in Cuba and had emigrated with his family from Havana as a young boy.

The Krome Avenue Center nestles at the edge of the Everglades, far from the bustle of Miami proper. Security is intense, with barbed wire enclosures within barbed wire laced corridors. Armed guards were posted at the gate and at check points inside.

We received visitor's tags, signed in at the reception desk and I submitted my shoulder bag for examination. It contained a pad, pens and my tape recorder. Finally, an officer arrived to personally escort us to the infirmary. We passed through a number of open courtyards and past several dormitories on our way, and everywhere we looked were detainees in bright orange jumpsuits milling about.

We were shown into an examining room with a desk and chairs, and Victor was brought to us. I was pleased that he immediately recognized me—the man with the white beard—as one of his rescuers. I introduced Rick, who set him at ease when he told him that they were from the same hometown, Havana. Rick explained that I was a writer and wanted to hear the whole story of the escape. Victor needed no prompting.

"I got the idea of escaping several years ago," he stated. "The situation in Cuba is terrible, especially for the young people.

There are no freedoms—no freedom to move about, no freedom of expression. We feel caged because there's no legal way to leave Cuba. There was only one way out; there were no alternatives.

"I had served my time in the Cuban Air Force and then gotten a job as a bus driver. Two months ago I was fired. My ideals, like those of so many other young people, were not compatible with the revolution.

"I lived alone in Havana in my own house, and early last month four friends and I decided to build a raft to escape. Each one was assigned a task. Different members of the group gathered individual items needed for building the raft for the trip. I was the leader. Of course, we all knew that if we were caught just gathering the materials to make a raft, we would receive a two-year prison sentence. We also knew that if we were caught at sea, it would mean 5 to 10 years. We didn't care. We had to escape.

"I bought the boards on the black market, and we sanded them smooth and drilled holes in them 10 centimeters apart for the ropes. We bolted two more boards crosswise to hold them together, and cut the front end to a sharp point, like the prow of a regular ship.

"I picked up three bus inner tubes at the bus depot for $15 apiece. It took several weeks, because I wanted brand new tubes, not old patched ones. We figured that the saltwater might dissolve patches. Then we inflated the tubes, wrapped them in burlap, and tied them on with heavy cord we had borrowed from some truck drivers we knew. Fortunately, with a little work, they fit on the boards. We hadn't measured the tires against the boards beforehand, so we were lucky everything fit together.

"Meanwhile, it took one of my buddies four weeks to locate a compass. We had to pay the equivalent in pesos of $200 for a diver's wrist compass. We had 10 small paddles made too, figuring that each of us should have a paddle, plus some spares. It would be easy to lose paddles at sea. The groceries were easy. We just went to the store and bought Russian canned goods.

"The whole time we were gathering parts and building the raft, we were terrified that we would be discovered. We did all the work inside my house and had to maintain careful security for fear the neighborhood (Communist) committee would discover what we were doing.

"When the raft was finally completed, however, the other

three guys took one look at the size of what we had built, thought about the miles of open ocean ahead of us—and chickened out. It's a good thing I had been thinking of someone else all along, although I had not said anything to him before. I would have made the trip alone, but I preferred to have at least one other guy along.

"I spoke to Joaquin Guillermo Gonzalez Cotto, a 22-year old acquaintance who did occasional construction work, and who I knew also wanted to escape Castro's 'prison.' He was afraid to join me until I explained that only one of three things could happen— we would die, we would go to jail or we would find freedom in the United States. Finally, he agreed, and I said that we would leave in two days, and not to mention a word to anyone.

"The next morning I caught a bus from Havana to Santa Cruz del Norte, about 40 miles east of the city. I wanted to case the beach from the highway that runs alongside the ocean. I had already arranged with a truck driver to carry us and our raft from the city to Santa Cruz at 9 o'clock the following night. The driver stood us up for an entire week, so I hired another driver who was willing to take the risk for $200—and he finally showed up the night of Friday, May 11.

"That evening we were scared to death. We didn't even dare to say goodbye to our families or anyone. Only the three friends who helped build the raft knew of our plans. As we each downed two shots of rum for courage, we got a lucky break. We had one of our frequent power failures at just the right time. All the lights in the neighborhood went out.

"When the driver arrived around 9 o'clock, we loaded the raft in his truck in the pitch dark and headed up the coast for Santa Cruz del Norte.

"When we reached the stretch of beach I thought I recognized from my earlier scouting trip on the bus, he quickly dumped us off alongside the highway and sped away in a big hurry. We were about 40 yards from the surf, with tall grass between us and the water, so we quickly dragged the heavy raft into the tall grass to inflate the inner tubes.

"When I looked around for the air pump, it wasn't there. In our panic, we had left it back at my house. As cars and trucks sped down the coastal highway a few yards away, we huddled in the grass and blew our lungs out trying to inflate the big bus inner tubes. I don't know how we did it, but an hour later, they were all filled solid. Then it took us another hour to haul the heavy raft through the tall grass some 40 yards to the water. Each time a car passed, we had to drop the raft and fall flat on the ground to keep from being seen.

"When we got to the water, my heart sank. We were not on a smooth sand beach. We were greeted by a wide stretch of sharp coral rocks, over which the surf crashed ominously in the darkness. This part of the coast has periodic stretches of such rocks between the areas of sandy beach. From the road, I had missed my mark, and now we had to launch the raft from where we found ourselves. It was too bulky to drag down the shoreline to a sandy stretch, and besides, the risk of being spotted was too great. Joaquin was terrified and I was pretty scared myself, but we tried to push off between the waves anyway.

"Nothing was going according to plan. The raging surf flung the raft over, and it smashed down on top of me, catching my right leg between the planking and the sharp coral rocks. My foot and leg were badly gashed, but I didn't realize just how badly until later.

"Despite the pain, I managed to right the raft and hold onto it, as the receding wave carried both me and the raft away from shore. I shouted to Joaquin to jump aboard, but he was petrified. He couldn't move and was wailing for his mother over the sound of the crashing surf. He didn't dare jump for a very simple reason—he couldn't swim.

"Here he was about to embark on a treacherous ocean voyage on three inner tubes, and he couldn't swim. As he clung to the slippery rocks in the swirling water, I managed to paddle back toward him, grab him by the arm, and drag him bodily into the raft.

"Miraculously, around midnight Friday night, we managed to paddle beyond the breakers. We had already lost six of our paddles and two of our water jugs, leaving only four paddles and three jugs on the raft. But we were finally on our way. Our ocean journey to freedom had begun at last. Immediately, we paddled with every ounce of strength we had to try to get out of sight of land by dawn.

"The sea was calm and a full moon cast a brilliant swathe across its surface. We could see the faint lights of a fisherman's longline about every 100 yards or so, but the only sound was the splashing from our frantic paddling.

"Just before first light, we heard two sudden bursts of machine

The "Catch" of A Lifetime

gun fire. We huddled low in terror, but nothing else happened, only silence. Evidently, the men on the gunboat hadn't actually seen us. Perhaps they were just shooting at the sound of our paddles in the darkness—or perhaps they were shooting at someone else nearby. We'll never know. All I know is that they disappeared as quickly as they came and we weren't hit. We waited awhile in breathless silence, then resumed paddling.

"When Saturday dawned, there was no sign of the gunboat, or any other boat for that matter, but we could still see the coast of Cuba in the distance. We continued paddling non-stop, but the constant exertion was already taking its toll. We were exhausted—and thirsty. By dawn we had already drunk one jug of water.

"Saturday morning I saw my first shark. Not just the first shark of the trip, but my very first shark. I had never been out on the ocean before and had only seen sharks in movies and books. He was only about three feet long, but we could feel him bump the raft beneath us. From then on, we no longer dangled our legs in the water, but rather crossed them uncomfortably in front of us.

"All day Saturday we paddled intermittently. The sun was intense, and we broiled in the scorching heat. By Saturday evening we had finished off our second jug of water.

"Saturday night the sea turned ugly. The wind began to howl and the waves got higher and higher. Soaked to the skin by giant breakers that constantly swept over our heads, we held on tight and shivered uncontrollably in the bitter cold of night. Two more paddles were washed away that night.

"Sunday morning the seas were still rough, and to make things worse, the cap on our third and last remaining water jug somehow wasn't screwed on tight when we stowed it after a morning swallow. As the rough seas tossed it about in the third inner tube, which we used for storage, it emptied out before we realized what had happened. We were out of water.

"Sunday was much like Saturday, scorching hot. We were too exhausted to paddle anymore and were resigned to just drift wherever the current would take us. We saw several distant ships. One even stopped about 500 yards from us, but then steamed off without acknowledging our waving and shouting. By Sunday afternoon, the sun and the sweltering heat began to get to us. I began to hallucinate that I was back home. Joaquin, too, was drifting in and out of consciousness as he began to give up hope.

"When we ran out of water, we didn't eat anymore. Although we had several cans of food left, the prospect of salty meat seemed worse than gnawing hunger. Most of all, we were tired. The cold and the seawater washing over us kept us from sleeping at night, and the overpowering heat kept us awake in the daytime.

"Sunday evening Joaquin said that he wanted to turn back. I explained that we couldn't paddle against the current, even if we tried. I convinced him that we had long since passed the point of no return and might just as well drift with the sea—and pray. We summoned up numerous saints, but it didn't seem to help. By late Sunday night we had resigned ourselves to death. We had no idea of where we were, and had about given up hope of being found. I told Joaquin that we would probably die, but at least we would die free.

"Monday dawned on the same endless expanse of ocean, and as if God were sending yet another trial upon us in our final hours, we had company. A giant black bird, I believe a frigate, kept swooping down on the raft and attacking us. We managed to beat it off with our two paddles, but in the process, lost one of them. We had little enough energy left, without expending it on a lousy bird.

"By mid-morning Monday, both our spirits and our bodies were totally drained. In desperation, we began to drink seawater. We knew the end was near.

"When the sun began to fall from its highest point, we spotted a small white boat in the distance. I wasn't sure if it saw us or not. We had already seen two big ships that morning, but they kept right on going, unaware of the presence of our little raft. The boat was heading straight toward us. As it drew closer, we could see that it had long poles sticking out from its sides. Finally, we could see men aboard, and when we waved and shouted to them, they shouted back, '¡Estados Unidos!' and threw us a jug of water. We were saved. We had survived to make a new life. We were free."

It was quite a story. According to officials I talked to, Victor was able to leave the detention center as soon as the ugly wounds on his foot and leg healed and he regained his strength. Joaquin was released soon after. When Rick and I visited him, he was all smiles.

Before we left him, he made a point of thanking me for saving his jacket. Although I didn't know it at the time, in the pocket he had stashed a soggy address book with the names, addresses and phone numbers of acquaintances and relatives in Miami. It was a very important little book to him.

Although his mother is still in Cuba, Victor has many relatives in the Miami area. Some of them visited the two young men at Krome a few days after they arrived. They assured them of a place to live until they were able to set out on their own in their new-found land of liberty.

Both Rick and I were emotionally drained from hearing Victor's account of his and Joaquin's ordeal. We marveled at the determination of one so young to endure such a voyage to freedom, knowing the terrible risks. I gave him my address and phone number and asked him to get in touch when he got settled. As I left, he once again poured out his gratitude for saving his life.

For all the years—make that decades—that I've been fishing offshore, I cannot think of a more satisfying "catch" than two such young men. The experience has given me a brand new perspective on the blessings we all enjoy in the "land of the free."

32

The Sportfishing Kayak

by Kevin Bartels

Most anglers set a hook in hopes that it will stick hard and fast, and not pull loose. As a general rule, calamity is a pulled hook. Well, not always. Recently, I prayed for a pulled hook, but it held fast, very nearly resulting in a calamity of a different sort. But let me start at the beginning.

A number of my friends and I own long, skinny, open-water kayaks, and we spend much of our free time racing each other in the waters near where we live on the island of Oahu in Hawaii. These boats are not the same as those usually seen in freshwater lakes and rivers. Such smaller craft are usually only about 10 to 12 feet long, while my open-water kayak measures 22 feet in length. Although it's streamlined and very light-weight for its length, paddling it for any great distance in offshore waters requires considerable stamina.

Those of us who own these boats take pride in the shape we're in, and our informal weekend races often become highly competitive. As part of my physical conditioning program, I often take my kayak out in the ocean by myself to paddle back and forth for hours at a time.

To make such activity more interesting, several of us have installed rodholders in our craft, so we can troll for supper while we paddle.

If you've ever seen a kayak of any kind, you'll know that there is very little room in the "cockpit" for anything but the paddler.

When I fish while I'm paddling, I take with me only my rod and reel, a small lure tied to my line, and a small cooler jammed into the limited space in front of my seat. There is no room for much of anything else, and, as it is, the cooler cramps my legs and feet.

On one such recent foray offshore, I launched my boat a little before noon. The weather was hot and sunny, and the seas flat calm. I planted my rod in the holder and let the line out to troll for whatever might bite.

By early afternoon I had caught three little papio, and put them in the small cooler at my feet. (In Hawaii we have our own names for all our local fish—most people would consider a papio similar to a jack crevalle.) I had developed a simple procedure for landing such small fish. After working them to the boat, I would tighten up on the drag, and from my seated position, lift them aboard. Of course, a net would have made things a good bit easier and reduced the risk of breaking them off, but as I said, there's very little space in a kayak for a full array of fishing equipment.

At mid-afternoon my rodtip bent sharply. I grabbed it and promptly hooked the fourth papio of the day. He fought gamely on the light rod, but he was outmatched, and within minutes I managed to reel him to the boat. I tightened the drag on my reel and was about to swing the fish into the cooler, when I noticed a dark shape rising up from beneath the struggling fish.

The next thing I knew, a five-foot hammerhead shark raised his head clear out of the water, snatched the little papio, and raced off with his free meal. As he turned and charged away from the boat with the hapless papio in his mouth, his tail slapped the side of the kayak, knocking my paddle into the water and nearly tipping me over.

Somehow, the hook on the jig was sticking out of the little papio's mouth just far enough to catch in the corner of the hammerhead's mouth. Since the shark hadn't swallowed the jig, his teeth weren't in a position to slice through the slender monofilament leader.

If I had wanted to catch a shark, Murphy's Law would have dictated that the leader would have been instantly severed by the shark's razor-sharp teeth. Since a five-foot hammerhead was the last thing in the world I wanted on the end of my line, of course everything held together. I was solidly hooked up.

Since the drag on my reel was tightened down hard, the shark

didn't strip any line from it. Rather, he began to slowly tow the light-weight kayak out to sea, and I had no choice but to hold on.

When the shark attacked the papio, I was no more than a quarter mile from shore. In no time at all, I had traveled a half mile out.

Of course, I could have let go of the rod and reel, but both were brand new, and I didn't want to lose them if I could help it. I had no knife or other means to simply cut the line, so I was faced with a tough decision.

About that time I noticed that the shark was not only towing the kayak farther and farther from shore, but we were approaching a shipping channel. I had almost decided to let the shark have my entire rig before he dragged me any farther out to sea.

Suddenly, the decision was made for me. My brand new Ugly Stik, which had been bent nearly double during the entire shark-ride, shattered in two places. As the fiberglass rod splintered, it severed the line.

At last I was free of the shark and I had at least saved my reel. However, there was yet another problem. My paddle, which had been knocked out of my hands when the shark first struck the papio, was floating off in the current a quarter mile away. The shark had indeed towed the boat a considerable distance.

I knew I couldn't make it to shore against the current by simply paddling the 22-foot kayak with my hands—and there was only one way I could retrieve the paddle.

I had to swim for it and tow the kayak behind me. The prospect of climbing into the water with a hammerhead that had just freed himself beneath my boat was not a happy one. The thought of swimming a full quarter mile in those same waters was even more unnerving.

But I had no choice. I slipped into the water as quietly as I could and towed the boat in the direction of the spot where the shark first began towing me. I tried to swim slowly and deliberately, without making any splashing sounds, for fear of drawing the shark back for another papio—or me.

Luckily, I found my paddle, and after counting my extremities, climbed back into the kayak. Fueled by the extra adrenalin generated by the experience, the paddle home was a breeze.

I simply told my buddies that I had to let the shark go free because it wouldn't fit in my little cooler.

Then I silently reminded myself to take a knife on future offshore fishing expeditions in my now-baptized sportfishing kayak.

33

Big Moe

by Capt. Randy Rode

axonomists call it *Sphyrna mokarran*. Most of us, however, call it by its common name, hammerhead shark. One particular great hammerhead, however, has yet a third name—Big Moe—and he visits us in the middle Florida Keys for a few weeks each spring. He is *not* welcome.

Hammerheads are fearsome creatures. They can attain a length of 20 feet, and their bulk is matched only by their nasty disposition. In fact, the first fatal shark attack ever recorded in American waters was by a great hammerhead off Long Island, New York, in 1815.

Hammerheads look as mean as they act, with great T-shaped heads and tall dorsal fins shaped exactly like everyone's nightmare vision of a traditional maneater. Their eyes are located at the ends of their hammer-shaped heads, and when they feed they sweep their broad, flat head back and forth in a scanning motion, the same way you would use a metal detector, in order to see what's in front of them.

Their favorite foods include stingrays, which they gobble with reckless abandon, poison barbs and all. They also relish oily fish such as mackerel and jacks—and tarpon. They love tarpon, which is how I've become so intimately acquainted with hammerhead sharks—and Big Moe in particular.

I've been a charter captain for most of my adult life, and have specialized in guiding clients to trophy tarpon for most of those years. Each spring, record class tarpon migrate to the waters surrounding the Florida Keys, and anglers pursue them with every-thing from heavy conventional tackle to light-weight flyrods. Their offerings range from large live baits to feather-weight flies.

Since many sportsmen favor light tackle, especially flyrods, fights with tarpon of more than 100 pounds often last hours. One doesn't whip such fish quickly with only the several pounds of drag allowed by light tippets or ultra-light lines. And as these great fish gradually tire, they become easy prey to the giant sharks that migrate with them on their trek southward along Florida's East Coast. Husky bull sharks and large hammerheads lead the list of predators that follow the tarpon, but one giant hammerhead in particular has been sighted repeatedly over the years in the area of the Bahia Honda bridges below Marathon in the middle Keys. He has been named "Big Moe."

My dad, Captain Dick Rode, remembers sighting this monster hammerhead as early as 1950, and I have spotted him virtually every year for the past 18 or 20 years, always between early and mid-April.

Oh, I know that there are those who scoff and claim that the sightings are not always of the same shark, but in my mind, I'm sure it's the same one. He's very distinctive—much larger and darker than other hammerheads. He's a dark brown, almost black, while most hammerheads are more of a dark yellow-brown color. He measures between 17 and 18 feet long, as estimated by com-paring his length against that of boats passing beside him. The consensus of dozens of guides and anglers is that he must weigh at least 1,000 pounds or more. His dorsal fin, too, is enormous, at least 30 inches high. It's higher than the gunnel of many of the boats that fish for tarpon around the Bahia Honda bridges. His eyes are the size of baseballs, and the distance between his eyes has been estimated at around six feet. He is a most monstrous fish.

Although most of the tarpon guides who fish the area of Bahia Honda feel that they have been seeing the same individual each year, an incident a few years ago clinched all subsequent identifi-cation. A guide, incensed at losing yet another trophy tarpon to the ravenous interloper, intentionally backed his skiff over him. His propeller blades cut distinctive diagonal scars on the shark's back, just behind his dorsal fin. Big Moe bears those easily recog-nizable scars to this day.

What is even more distinctive about Big Moe is his ability to eat giant tarpon. The mouths of hammerheads are small when compared to the massive size of their bodies, and only a giant member of the species can wrap his mouth around the fat mid-section of a trophy-size tarpon. Smaller sharks have difficulty penetrating the large, hard scales of a tarpon, which protect this prize gamefish from the teeth of smaller predators. Big Moe has no trouble at all biting through the tarpon's natural armor.

Big Moe's predations became so predictable and devastating that the Marathon Tarpon Tournament went so far as to change its dates from April to May several years ago, because of Big Moe's annual April appearances.

Every year around that time one guide or another has a run-in with Big Moe, losing a client's trophy catch to the insatiable monster. I've had my share of run-ins, heaven knows, but some years ago I very nearly got my revenge.

Several macho, football-player types showed up at the dock at-

that time. They were all in their 20s and built like weight-lifters, and they wanted to fish for sharks—"big sharks."

I told them I could oblige, but as they watched me load the boat with my shark-fishing gear, some of their "macho" attitude dissipated. I must admit the equipment was impressive: 14/0 Penn Senators loaded with 130-pound test Dacron line and mounted on heavy rods, coils of #19 leader wire; bang sticks and a box of shotgun shells, a coil of aircraft cable, crimping tools and sleeves, big, reinforced flying gaffs, tail ropes, buoys, heavy harnesses, and the largest hooks those boys had ever seen.

As I mounted the big fighting chair onto the pedestal, I declared that we were going after Big Moe. "Yeah!" these big, tough guys hooted.

We anchored up alongside the old Bahia Honda bridge. Actually, the Bahia Honda bridge is two bridges. The new one is about 10 years old. The other, now closed to all traffic, was originally built early this century as part of Henry Flagler's railroad route between the mainland of Florida and Key West. When the great hurricane of 1926 destroyed most of the railroad, several bridges remained intact, and they became the base for part of the highway that was subsequently built over the same route. This highway that hops over and between the islands of the Keys spans many miles of open ocean. Beneath its bridges and around their pilings, record-class tarpon swarm each spring, pausing in their migratory wanderings.

Once anchored, I skewered a dead 40-pound tarpon on three giant hooks secured to each other with a heavy steel (#19) leader wire. This was to be our shark bait. (This was before the state law was passed requiring a $50 tag to kill a tarpon.) One hook was in the jaw, one in the belly, and one stuck in the tail. Then, I crimped a 20-foot leader of 500-pound-test steel aircraft cable onto the lead hook and set out a chum bag full of ground fish, with some menhaden oil added to "sweeten" it. We all sat back to await our guest diner, Big Moe.

No guests at all showed up, much less Big Moe. I reeled the bait back to the boat, butterflied it, removed the backbone, and set it back out again. This time I tied on four large lobster trap floats at the swivel clip, to float the bait off the bottom.

The fish oil was pouring out its message all the while, and shortly a giant fin appeared, circling the bait. Judging from its size, there was no doubt it belonged to Big Moe. For 15 minutes he circled the floats, his great dorsal standing three feet above the surface of the water. My anglers watched slack-jawed, their bravado by now reduced to silent mutterings of "awesome."

Finally, the giant shark moved up on the tarpon and swallowed the entire fish. As I set the hook, the shark disappeared beneath the surface, dragging the four large styrofoam floats with him. For a full half hour we didn't see those floats again. Line screamed from the big reel, and we followed the fish around the bridge pilings several times, then under the seaward bridge, and finally out to sea.

That shark dragged us past Hawk's Channel some five miles from our starting point. After two hours of tug-of-war, one angler, exhausted, gave up, and was replaced by his fresher companion. That one only lasted an hour before the third young man took his turn at the rod.

Big Moe was tiring, too, and he began to thrash at the surface, shaking his massive head from side to side, and (I swear) staring at us with first one eye, then the other, from the ends of his grotesque head. Then, not as tired as we thought he was, he made yet another 200-yard run against the heavy drag.

What none of us aboard knew, however, was that when he initially grabbed the bait, he swallowed *all three hooks*. The heavy steel cable had been grating over his sharp teeth for three long hours. During that time, he severed the individual strands of the cable leader one by one, until finally he sliced through the last one. Three and a half hours after hookup and over five miles at sea, the heavy cable parted, and Big Moe escaped to fight again another day. We had met the enemy—and lost.

My anglers hadn't landed the giant shark they were seeking, but they were mightily impressed and happy about the experience. As far as I know, that was the only time Big Moe has ever been hooked.

Several years later, I had my hairiest encounter of all with Big Moe, and this time *he* had the upper hand.

It was mid-April, and a couple of gentlemen from Iowa chartered me for what turned out to be their very first saltwater fishing experience. What an initiation they got!

At four in the afternoon I picked up a couple of dozen live mullet and we headed for Bahia Honda in my 25-foot center console

Pacemaker All Glass. They joked that our baits were larger than anything they had ever caught before in their lives.

The weather was hot and humid and the seas were slick calm. It promised to be a beautiful evening. The timing was perfect. I anchored with a breakaway anchor on the up-current side of the new bridge and set out the baits into a moderate outgoing tide. We all relaxed and waited for the tarpon to show up.

About seven o'clock, with the sun dropping fast on the horizon, the great silver fish began to feed. We immediately hooked a beauty of about 100 pounds, turned loose the breakaway anchor, and cranked up to keep the fish from getting into the bridge pilings. He made it before I could stop him, however, so I let my two anglers off on the bridge cap. I loosened the drag on the reel, and then instructed them to pass the rod beneath the crossbeam between the two bridge caps. Once the line was free of the obstruction, I hollered for them to move to the seaward side of the cap. When I picked them up on the other side, the fish was still on.

After successfully preventing a cutoff on the bridge pilings, I once again tightened the drag on the reel, and my angler continued to fight the fish in the waters between the two bridges. Everything was going perfectly, although my two anglers figured that they had experienced a lifetime of excitement already.

The tarpon was beginning to tire from the heavy pressure of the stiff rod and heavy drag. It was then that I saw the tall dorsal fin, cutting the slick surface as it approached from the new bridge. The fin made little ripple lines in the water that spread behind it like a tiny wake.

I shouted "Big Moe's coming to get your tarpon. Let's get him in *fast!*" I explained that Big Moe was a 1,000-pound hammerhead, but they didn't believe me at first—until they saw the fin.

They let out a scream like you've never heard. "My God, look at the size of him." Their eyes got as big as dinner plates, as they watched Big Moe move straight in on the tired tarpon.

I don't know how that tarpon summoned the energy, but he took off greyhounding against the drag of that 50-pound class reel, with Moe right on top of him. I put the boat in a hard circle and gunned the engines wide open, to try to scare the shark off the fish long enough for us to land him. It sometimes works with smaller, less aggressive sharks, but it made no impression at all on Big Moe.

The next thing we saw was Big Moe with his whole head out of

Big Moe

the water, clutching the 100-pound tarpon sideways in his mouth. The 6-foot tarpon barely stretched the full distance between Big Moe's eyes.

Evidently, however, Moe didn't have a good hold on the tarpon, and it wriggled out of his grasp. The shark went crazy—his meal was escaping.

The tarpon, nobody's fool, immediately swam underneath our boat. I shouted to my angler to drop the rodtip down into the water, and as he did so, the tarpon popped up on the other side of the boat. For several seconds, we couldn't see the shark, but we could see the tarpon swimming slowly. He was bleeding from his midsection and missing a bunch of scales.

All of a sudden, we felt something bump the boat beneath our feet; then Big Moe erupted on the other side and grabbed the tarpon a couple of feet from the side of the boat. The shark had blue bottom paint all over his dorsal fin and the top of his back. The angler, who hadn't yet turned the fighting chair around to face the fish, was now *pushing* on the rod, which was bent backwards, over his head. Line was screaming from the reel.

When he finally turned the chair, we could all see a 24-inch bite missing from the tarpon's stomach. The poor fish was laying on the surface, quivering. We watched Big Moe swing around once again and eat that tarpon right up to its head.

The angler reeled in the 35-pound tarpon head and it was all over. The ripples died out over the slick surface of the water, and a twilight sun shone red above the horizon.

It was still prime tarpon-fishing time, and my anglers were gradually calming down. One client still wanted his trophy. He wanted a mounted tarpon to hang over his bar back home, and a head mount just wouldn't do. I headed back to my anchor float.

Once again, I set out a live bait, all the while scanning the area for signs of shark. Sure enough, I could see Big Moe's giant dorsal fin cutting the water about 100 yards away, but evidently, his recent meal was holding him.

In a matter of minutes, we hooked up again, and this time we got the tarpon to the boat *fast*. As I lip-gaffed the fish, I looked up and saw Big Moe swimming straight for the boat. I hastily roped the fish through the mouth and gills, hauled him half out of the water, cinched the rope to a cleat, and then hauled anchor as fast as I could.

Complete Angler's Library

Big Moe

As I cranked up the engines and gunned the boat away from the spot, I turned to see Big Moe reaching out of the water, trying to grab the tarpon above the waterline. We sped off with our trophy intact, as Big Moe missed grabbing his second free meal by scant inches.

There is no reason not to believe that as long as anglers fight trophy tarpon in the shadow of the Bahia Honda bridges each April, Big Moe will continue to pick off these tired giants as they're being reeled to the boat. Age doesn't seem to have diminished his resolve to grab a free meal whenever he can, and the excitement he generates almost matches that of catching giant tarpon on light tackle.

34

The "Terriblest" Way to Die

by Don Mann

Children, however sugar-and-spicy, often play macabre mind games. I can remember one in particular from my own childhood, scores of years ago. It was a rainy Sunday afternoon, and several young friends and I had exhausted our patience on a game of Monopoly. We became embroiled in a heated debate over which of all possible deaths was most horrible. As I recall, our term was "terriblest."

As only children blessed with a peculiar wisdom born of vivid imaginations can do, we argued the relative merits of death by fire, drowning, hanging, and shooting. Various calibers even drew heated argument. Deadly spider and scorpion bites, attacks by ferocious jungle beasts, and terminal frostbite incurred in a raging blizzard at one Pole or the other also drew spirited advocacy.

Although we concurred that to die in our sleep was our unanimous preference, the discussion of the "terriblest" way to die spurred heated debate. In retrospect, it was a grisly discussion.

I vividly remember settling the matter, however, when I announced that to be eaten alive by a giant, man-eating shark was my idea of the "most terriblest" way to die. All other forms of mayhem paled in comparison, and my companions, silenced by the mere thought, nodded in complete agreement.

With such a decision having been made at so early an age, you can imagine the feeling in my stomach when I opened my morning newspaper the other day to read the headline, "Feet Found in Tiger Shark."

The headline didn't exaggerate. It seems that a North Florida shark fisherman, Jess Dick, the captain of the commercial fishing vessel, the *Patricia Anne*, landed an eight-foot, 350-pound tiger shark 23 miles off Amelia Island. While he was removing the beast's innards, he made a grisly discovery—in the shark's stomach was a pair of size 8 ½ Ocean Pacific high-top sneakers. What's worse, one sneaker contained an entire adult foot, and the other contained a sock and some bits of skin.

A Coast Guard boat was immediately dispatched to pick up the gruesome remains, which it delivered to a medical examiner in Jacksonville, Florida. The examiner said that although the foot showed signs of being severed by a shark, her office had no way of telling whether the shark killed the victim or if the victim was already dead when the shoes, and feet, were swallowed. Neither possibility was a pleasant one.

If there was ever a garbage eater in the sea, it's a tiger shark. They have been known to eat just about anything. The list of things found in tiger shark stomachs reads like the inventory of an entire flea market: lumps of coal, cans, books, nuts and bolts, lobsters, boat cushions, conch shells, wads of baling wire, a wallet, driftwood, the hind leg of a sheep, the head of a crocodile, other sharks—and human limbs.

I once took a break from fishing while anchored off north Key Largo with my son. We consumed a half-bucket of fried chicken and threw the bones over our shoulders into the shallow waters over the reef. When we resumed fishing, we caught a young tiger shark.

Later, back at the dock, I held our trophy up by the tail for my son to take a snapshot. As I hoisted the fish off the ground, the shark's stomach emptied its contents. Before our eyes lay *every* single chicken bone we had tossed into the sea, plus some heavy wire and a foot-square piece of cowhide. The tiger shark is truly the garbage collector of the sea.

The discovery of the sneakers was not even a first. Some years earlier, the stomach of a 300-pound tiger caught off South Florida yielded an Adidas hightop sneaker—plus a human leg bone.

Although not really considered aggressive, tiger sharks are dangerous simply because they will eat anything they find in front of them. Why they deviate from their regular diet of turtles, fish, and sea birds is a mystery, but examination of their stomach con-

The "Terriblest" Way To Die

tents attests to their consistently omnivorous eating habits.

Unlike the owner of the south Florida sneaker, the owner of the pair of Ocean Pacifics has been tentatively identified as one of three fishermen lost at sea over 40 miles from the spot where the tiger shark was caught.

Nearly a month earlier, three friends set out for a day's fishing from a public ramp near Jacksonville, Florida. They launched their 22-foot-long boat early on a Friday morning and were expected home by about nine that evening. They never returned.

The following day their boat was found about 12 miles southeast of the entrance to the St. Johns River. It was overturned and still anchored, but there was no sign of the three men in the area. Officials had no way of knowing what caused the boat to capsize, and until the boat was found, had not the slightest idea of where to look for the missing men. They had not filed a float plan before setting out for their day's fishing trip. An operations officer with the Coast Guard was quoted as saying, "We spent the first 13 hours looking all over the place."

All that weekend Coast Guard, Navy, and police officials, as well as private and commercial boaters searched the waters off Jacksonville and south Georgia. Friends and officials searched through the nights in boats, while aerial searchers helped scan the seas during the daytime.

Finally, about 1:30 p.m. on Monday, one body wearing a life jacket was found in the ocean 29 miles east of Cumberland Island and about 41 miles from where the boat had been found two days earlier. It had been nearly three days since the three men had first been reported missing. The body was flown by helicopter to the Jacksonville Naval Air Station, where it was positively identified as one of the missing fishermen. The search for the other two then intensified in the area where the body had been found.

Tuesday, a helicopter pilot spotted a floating life jacket 31 miles east of Jekyll Island, Georgia, but the jacket turned out to be from a commercial vessel. Nothing else was sighted that day.

Tuesday night, the Coast Guard and the Navy called off the official search. They had scoured 11,650 square miles of the Atlantic since the search began, and by Tuesday evening, after four days of intense effort, they gave up hope of finding the other two alive.

Friends of the missing men and sympathetic volunteers in pri-

The "Terriblest" Way To Die   245

vate planes continued to search farther north along the Georgia coast for several more days, but their efforts proved fruitless. They too finally gave up.

Later that week, the Jacksonville Medical Examiner's Office announced that the man whose body had been found Tuesday had apparently drowned sometime Sunday night, about 12 hours before his body was found. He had apparently been alive for two whole days since the boat overturned and had been drifting slowly northward in the current.

It was fully two and a half weeks later when the commercial shark fisherman hauled the giant tiger shark aboard his boat, gutted his catch, and found the pair of high-topped sneakers. If there is any positive aspect to the story, it's that at least his relatives won't have to spend the rest of their days wondering if he might still be alive somewhere.

As I read the chilling account in the newspaper, my mind wandered back to those macabre childhood debates of so many decades ago. The immature imaginings of one so young, one who had never seen death before, had been right on the mark.

To be eaten by a giant shark just had to be the absolute worst way to die.